COOKING THE WILD SOUTHWEST

Delicious Recipes for Desert Plants
COOKING THE WILD SOUTHWEST

CAROLYN NIETHAMMER

ILLUSTRATIONS BY **PAUL MIROCHA**

THE UNIVERSITY OF ARIZONA PRESS / TUCSON

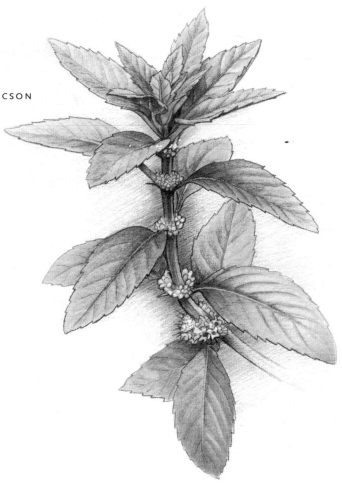

Neither the author nor the University of Arizona Press will accept responsibility for any ill-
ness, injury, or death resulting from misidentification of desert plants used in this book.
Those readers who elect to gather such plants should take special care to check them against
a standard guide to regional flora. State and local regulations for gathering plants, seeds, and
fruits on public lands vary widely; readers are therefore strongly urged to seek guidance from
the appropriate authorities before collecting. Of course, any collecting on private property
must be done with the permission of the owner of that property.

The University of Arizona Press
© 2011 Carolyn J. Niethammer
All rights reserved
www.uapress.arizona.edu

Library of Congress Cataloging-in-Publication Data
Niethammer, Carolyn J.
Cooking the wild Southwest : delicious recipes for desert plants / Carolyn J. Niethammer.
    p. cm.
Includes bibliographical references and index.
ISBN 978-0-8165-2919-3 (pbk. : alk. paper)
1. Cooking, American—Southwestern style. 2. Cookbooks. I. Title.
TX715.2.S69N558 2011
641.5979—dc23   2011017003

Manufactured in the United States of America on acid-free, archival-quality paper
containing a minimum of 30% postconsumer waste and processed chlorine free.

16   15   14   13   12   11   6   5   4   3   2   1

For Susan Adler,

WHO KNOWS WHAT A FRIEND SHOULD BE

CONTENTS

Fruits, Flowers, and Cactus Pads

Nuts, Pods, and Seeds

Wild Greens

Flavorings from the Wild

TABLES

ACKNOWLEDGMENTS

It may take a village to raise a child, and most authors would agree it takes a village full of experts, friends, and friends of friends to write a book.

At the beginning of this project, Gary Paul Nabhan sent me to several important documents and to Penny "Piñon Penny" Frazier. Teacher and food entrepreneur Martha "Muffin" Burgess gave me a recipe for chia and told me about Mark Moody, who's entered the mesquite world with great zeal as a grower and mesquite-meal producer. Brent Bolton sent me to Al and Jane Smoake, who contributed some recipes and told me the story of how their town of Socorro, New Mexico, got behind their fledgling local food enterprise. Susan Adler shared her delicious chia breakfast parfait and told me that Johanna Stryker-Smit had substituted barrel cactus fruits in one of my coffee-cake recipes with great results. When I missed the acorn and sumac seasons, Julie Szekely introduced me to Chuck LeFevre, who generously gave me bags of products he'd saved as a by-product of his seed business. Martha Blue took me to meet ethnobotanist Phyllis Hogan one beautiful summer day in Flagstaff, Arizona.

I went to Linda McKittrick for advice on using chiltepines and found a friend and fellow food enthusiast who joyfully accompanied me on further adventures with elderberry flowers and cholla buds. John Dicus, grower of delicious prickly pear pads at Rivenrock Gardens in Nipomo, California, is always a good source of information on all things prickly pear. Mary Paganelli of Tohono O'odham Community Action (TOCA) gave information on Tohono O'odham products.

The ever-gracious Cheri Romanoski of Cheri's Desert Harvest provided some recipes, as did professional chef Molly Beverly of Prescott College's Crossroads Café; Eric Flatt, owner, and Aaron Geister, head chef, of Tonto Bar and Grill in Cave Creek, Arizona; John Sharpe, chef and owner of the Turquoise Room in Winslow, Arizona; and Doug Levy of Feast in Tucson. My husband, Ford Burkhart, was always happy to taste-test the recipes, and was adventurous in eating that day's experiment for lunch or dinner, especially if it was cake.

And we are all indebted to Wendy Hodgson for her decades of work on *Food Plants of the Sonoran Desert*, which includes many plants that grow throughout the Southwest.

Finally, I would like to thank the folks at University of Arizona Press who thought it was time after twenty-four years to consider an update of *Tumbleweed Gourmet*, my earlier look at edible desert plants. I am especially grateful to the copy editor, Debra Makay, who made sure all the ingredients were there and properly measured and the instructions made sense. Any errors or omissions are entirely my own.

INTRODUCTION

When I began researching edible desert plants in 1970, I learned that since time immemorial, mesquite pods have been the staple of the Native Americans who lived in my part of the Sonoran Desert. They grew a little corn, but the rainfall was too spotty and too unreliable to count on corn to get them through the year.

To learn more about mesquite, I spent an afternoon with two very generous middle-aged Tohono O'odham women at the San Xavier Indian Reservation outside Tucson. I arrived with a bag full of mesquite pods I'd gathered. I can't remember how we ground the pods, probably with a hand-turned food mill, but at the end of the afternoon we had a meal that we cooked with water to produce a not-unpleasant mesquite mush. This is what their grandmothers had made for them and they hadn't had any in decades. For centuries, maybe millennia, simple mesquite porridge was the staple of their ancestors. In the mid-twentieth century, there were no doubt other Indians around the Southwest who were still making the occasional pot of mesquite porridge, but by that time it was pretty much a forgotten food.

Contrast that with the autumn of 2009. In preparation for testing the recipes for this book, I had filled two five-gallon buckets with mesquite pods. The day before, I had spread them out on the patio, picked out the twigs, and looked the pods over for black mold and other discoloration. Then I sprayed them off with a sharp blast from the hose and let them dry.

The next day I took them to a mill only a few blocks from my house. I'm fortunate that every fall Desert Harvesters sets up their hammermill in a nearby neighborhood. For a modest fee, they'll take your mesquite pods, grind them in the hammermill, and return to you a finely ground tasty flour. The inedible husks and shells are magically sifted out. I got there just as they opened for business at 9 a.m. and already there were twenty-four people in line ahead of me, some of them with six and seven buckets of pods. (Five gallons of whole pods will produce a gallon of fine mesquite meal.) As I waited my turn, more people were driving up and the line lengthened down the block. None of these folks were Native American. The local Tohono O'odham have their own hammermill on the reservation serving those who have seen the wisdom of going back to the old ways. So the group that autumn morning represented new converts to desert foods. Meanwhile, in the community garden nearby, volunteers were flipping mesquite pancakes to round out the carnival atmosphere of the morning.

A New Interest in Eating Local Food

In the last few decades, interest in eating locally has exploded—whether it is New Jersey residents snapping up just-picked peaches and corn at farmers' markets or desert dwellers in the Southwest taking a new look at prickly pear and mesquite, many of us are beginning to pay more attention to the origin of our food.

In the Southwest, Native Seeds/SEARCH, located in Tucson, has led the way since 1983. They have rescued many desert-adapted heritage foods from the brink of extinction. An annual catalog now offers seeds for the ancient crops and their wild relatives. Desert Harvesters, also in Tucson, has concentrated mainly on educating residents on how to plant and raise mesquite trees using water harvesting techniques and then use the nutritious pods the trees produce.

Detailing all the local groups spread over the United States would be a book in itself. A successful example is the Southern Foodways Alliance. In 1999, a group of fifty southerners got together in Birmingham, Alabama, and formed the alliance. This 800-member group documents, studies, and celebrates the diverse food cultures of the changing American South. They conduct oral histories, make documentary films, host events, and publish a series called *Cornbread Nation*, featuring the best of southern food writing.

Building on their success, in 2008 a similar group of westerners formed Sabores sin Fronteras/Flavors without Borders, a regional, binational, and multicultural alliance to document, celebrate, and conserve farming and food folkways that span the U.S./Mexico borderlands from Texas and Tamaulipas on the east to California and Baja California on the west.

Within that area is the Santa Cruz Valley Heritage Alliance, which works to celebrate and promote the wild foods and agricultural products of the Santa Cruz Valley. The valley, which runs roughly from Marana north of Tucson to the Mexican border at Nogales, has an agricultural heritage going back more than 4,000 years, making it possibly the longest continually cultivated region in the United States.

Also within that area is the Tohono O'odham Community Action (TOCA) group, dedicated to creating a healthy and sustainable community on the Tohono O'odham Nation. Among its many programs, TOCA promotes traditional foods, grows native crops, and gives cooking classes. It also operates the Desert Rain Café, offering local foods to residents of the community of Sells as well as travelers and visitors. Each dish contains at least one traditional product.

Ecology leaders in New Mexico calling themselves "bioneers" have organized Dreaming New Mexico, a project to look ahead to a more equitable and sustainable food system for all the state's residents. The organizers have identified six agro-ecoregions and within them are looking at foodsheds, food security, preservation of farmlands, and biocultural legacies, which include the wild foods of the area.

These changes in food awareness aren't happening just in the United States—which seems to be the center of the universe for fast and overly processed food. The international slow food movement started in 1986 in Italy as a protest against a McDonald's that was to be opened in Rome. The organization, which celebrates traditional foods, now has more than 100,000 members in 132 countries.

As our awareness of the joys and health benefits of local foods has increased, we have adopted a whole new lexicon. We speak of someone as a "locavore," a person who seeks out foods that are grown and produced within a 100- to 250-mile radius. The term was coined in 2005 by a San Francisco group and was the New Oxford American Dictionary word of the year for 2007.

Another word we've been hearing frequently is "foodshed." That's been around since the early-twentieth century, but its usage is now expanding. Your foodshed refers to everything between where a food is produced and where a food is consumed—the land it grows on, the routes it travels, the markets it goes through, the kitchens where it is cooked. For most Americans, their foodshed is the entire globe—grapes from Chile, wine from Australia, pineapples from Hawaii, olive oil from Italy—not a very sustainable way to live.

A Growing Base of Literature

The last few years have also given us numerous books examining our modern eating behavior and suggesting better ways to put dinner on the table. Barbara Kingsolver in *Animal, Vegetable, Miracle* describes how her family, living on a small farm in Appalachia, spent a year eating only what they could grow or buy from others who produced it locally. While they did miss some things, they ate very well from their lush ecosystem. Gary Paul Nabhan set a more challenging task for himself, attempting for a year to eat most of his meals from ingredients sourced within 200 miles of his home in Tucson in the Sonoran Desert.

For a look at the diverse food traditions across our country, we can thank RAFT (Renewing America's Food Traditions), an affiliate of Slow Food USA. RAFT is an alliance of food, farming, environmental, and culinary advocates who have joined together to identify, restore, and celebrate America's biologically and culturally diverse food traditions. They are attempting to do that through conservation, education, and regional networking. In addition to their main compendium, *Savoring and Saving the Continent's Most Endangered Foods*, edited by Nabhan, RAFT has published a series of small books highlighting local foodways. So far they have covered Salmon Nation in the Northwest and Bison Nation in the Great Plains and produced publications on the food traditions of New England, the Great Lakes areas, and California.

Michael Pollan has written several books documenting our national food production and consumption habits and finding them very worrisome. For Pollan the situation is not simply one of better flavor, organic growing methods, and knowing your farmer. He sees the problem as much deeper. In a June 2010 essay in the *New York Review of Books* he writes:

> For some in the [food] movement, the more urgent problem is environmental: the food system consumes more fossil fuel energy than we can count on in the future (about a fifth of the total American use of such energy) and emits more greenhouse gas than we can afford to emit, particularly since agriculture is the one human system that *should* be able to substantially rely on photosynthesis: solar energy. It will be difficult if not impossible to address the issue of climate change without reforming the food system.

A Better Way of Eating

Consider that in our modern high-input farm system, it takes about 10 calories of fossil fuel energy to produce 1 calorie of supermarket food. This is astounding considering that in your backyard you can grow a simple vegetable garden with a few seeds and water, which you have to pay for, and dirt and sunshine, which are free. If your dirt isn't good enough for a garden, you can make it better with free compost you can make yourself from your vegetable scraps, your coffee grounds, and manure that you can also acquire for free. The National Gardening Association expected 43 million American households to grow their own fruits, vegetables, herbs, and berries in 2010, a 19 percent increase over the previous year.

Even easier to put on your table are the wild foods in this book. They are all simple to recognize; there's very little chance of poisoning yourself with the wrong thing. Mother Nature takes care of the planting, the fertilizing, and the watering. You do the gathering and the cooking. Couldn't be less complicated.

This book discusses 23 wild foods found in the arid Southwest, all planted and tended by Mother Nature. But that's only a fraction of what's out there. Wendy Hodgson, in her exhaustive book *Food Plants of the Sonoran Desert,* documents 540 edible plants used by people of more than 50 traditional cultures of the Sonoran Desert and peripheral areas. She writes that of the scrubby, sometimes sparse plants in this part of the Southwest, fully one-fifth are edible. Of course the plants in Hodgson's book are not the only edible plants in the Southwest. Additional plants are found in other, different ecosystems throughout the area.

While such foods as wild greens, acorns, and prickly pear pads once had the whiff of "poor people's food" about them, today they are relished and on the cutting edge of gastronomy. The Southwest's most inventive chefs feature them on their menus. For southwesterners, these foods are our *goût de terroir,* a French term that can be translated as "taste of the earth."

I'm not advocating adopting an all-wild-foods diet. We're too many out here in the West and we can't devote all our time to food gathering and processing. But some plants are easy to gather and plentiful. Millions of mesquite pods are raked up and dumped in landfills every summer, so there's plenty of room for increased use. And although many wild creatures subsist on prickly pear fruits, there are thousands of acres of them out there, many of which dry up and fall to the ground. Even if you didn't go out to gather *bellotas* (Emory acorns) yourself, you could pay somebody to do that for you while you enjoy the acorns and help to maintain that food tradition.

Nor am I suggesting that we go back to eating the mesquite mush the Tohono O'odham women taught me to make. It certainly is healthy—it just isn't the way we eat today. But all of these heritage foods can be incorporated into our present way of eating—and that is the purpose of this book.

We can also use modern cooking techniques as we transform these wild foods into breakfast or dinner. Actually, the seed for the original version of this book was planted in my mind by a Zuni woman while I was researching my first cookbook. I was asking her about a special Zuni sauce that was traditionally made by smashing together onions, garlic, and ground cherries on a stone mortar.

"Do you still make that?" I asked.

"Oh, yes," my Zuni friend told me, "but now I use my blender."

As the Zuni woman had indicated, no rule says you have to use ancient techniques in preparing ancient foods. Blenders, food processors, and slow cookers can make quick work of what took Indian and settler women all day. In other words, it is not necessary to go to a streambed and pound mesquite pods with a 20-pound pestle in a bedrock mortar.

Realistically, we cannot expect all the inhabitants of such Sunbelt cities as Tucson, Phoenix, Indio, Albuquerque, and Austin to head for the weed patch every night after work to gather their supper. But even a small movement in the direction of eating local can make a big difference.

The Leopold Center for Sustainable Agriculture found that the average fresh food item on American dinner tables now travels 1,500 miles to get there. While you may not have the time to supply all your needs from your garden or the wild, were you to add just some local foods to your diet you would greatly reduce the average distance traveled and energy consumption per meal. Even a small effort can make a big difference. In Barbara Kingsolver's *Animal, Vegetable, Miracle,* Steven L. Hopp writes: "If every U.S. citizen ate just one meal a week composed of locally and organically raised meats and produce, we would reduce our country's oil consumption by over 1.1 million barrels (not gallons) of oil every week."

Including some of these delicious and easily available plants in our diets even once in a while can keep us connected to our beautiful and generous Southwest homeland, which is willing to nurture us in ways we have forgotten.

Sustainable Harvesting

When you go out to gather wild foods, treat the desert and the plants with respect. Hook the saguaro fruits down with a pole; don't throw stones at them or any other cactus. When you find a stand of plants you wish to gather, take only a portion and leave the rest for the animals and to propagate more plants. Don't pull plants up by the roots; trim off what you need with scissors or a knife.

Watch where you are stepping—don't trample baby plants that might be growing under the adults. They are the food of tomorrow!

Nutrition

There has to be a reason why someone would go to the time and expense of running a nutritional test on a food. This reason is usually economic. Since only a few of these plants are sold commercially, nutritional information isn't always available. Ruth Greenhouse of the Desert Botanical Garden in Phoenix conducted some analyses for her 1979 master's thesis, and both Wendy Hodgson and Gary Paul Nabhan have published nutritional information where it exists. I have included whatever nutritional information I could find for each plant. Sometimes there was nothing I could locate.

The Recipes

I have developed, adapted, or borrowed all of the recipes here. I have tested practically all of them—in the rare case that I did not actually cook it myself, that is noted. I have fed everything to my husband or my guests, enlisting them as taste testers. You must have an adventurous palate to invite me to a potluck when I'm writing a cookbook like this—I guarantee I won't arrive with an ordinary potato salad.

I understand that gathering wild foods takes considerable time and organization to get into the field at the perfect time for picking a plant. In the case of saguaro fruits, you are getting up before dawn because you are doing your gathering when it's really hot out. Because I know how much energy goes into the harvest, I want to make sure that each recipe you use produces something delicious.

In the case of prickly pear or saguaro fruit or mesquite or tepary beans, this is never a problem. It is the rare person who doesn't like those flavors. Other flavors, such as that of bellotas (Emory acorns), don't appeal to everyone. If you don't like the underlying flavor, you would be disappointed in anything you make incorporating that ingredient.

The number of recipes is not balanced over the chapters—there are many more suggestions for mesquite and prickly pear than for acorns. This reflects partially the perceived palatability to the greatest number of people, but mostly the abundance and ease of gathering the ingredients.

If you start the year with two or three gallons of mesquite meal, you'll be interested in a greater variety of recipes for mesquite than for the tiny handful of wild mint leaves you may have collected.

Most of the recipes using these wild foods do include additional ingredients from outside the area—that is the nature of the way Americans eat. A cookbook focusing on a true locavore diet would appeal to some, and might be a project for the future. But for this book, my focus is on expanding the number of people who enjoy desert foods as part of their diet.

The little anecdotes I sometimes share regarding how I came upon a recipe are there simply to illustrate that these recipes did not appear full-blown to me in a dream. I made them up and so can you. If I tasted something or saw a recipe in a magazine or newspaper that seemed like it would be good with one of the wild foods, I tried it; if it turned out all right, I added it to my files. There is always room for improvement, however, and I hope that the better cooks among my readers will waste no time in doing some tinkering with these recipes.

So to all of you whose idea of cooking with desert foods begins and ends with prickly pear jelly, I offer this introduction to the incredible bounty of our southwestern deserts and the recipes to help you put them on your table. Bon appétit! Buen provecho!

Fruits, Flowers, and Cactus Pads

Prickly Pear

To the two-legged desert rat, the spicy, fruity odor of a deep red sun-warmed prickly pear is as much a herald of the coming autumn as the fragrance of ripening apples is for midwesterners. Native Americans have always considered the prickly pear a seasonal addition to their diet, but for Anglos its use has been largely confined to prickly pear jelly, a pleasant-tasting spread more exotic sounding than it really is. That is unfortunate, for when creatively used in recipes such as those that follow, the prickly pear is a delightful fruit with a tangy sweetness and an enticing color. Both the pads and the fruits offer important health benefits (see below).

Although prickly pears are now found around the globe, they are a New World plant. Native populations throughout the Southwest have relied on prickly pear for millennia and welcomed its sweetness. The tribes had distinctive methods of collecting the pads and the fruits and varied ways of preparing them. The fruits are easily gathered and when there were more than could be consumed fresh, they were dried or made into syrup for storage.

Columbus took the plant back to Europe at the end of the fifteenth century and from there it has spread all over the planet. When the Spanish explorers took the plants to Spain, it wasn't so much for the prickly pear itself but for the cochineal insects that feed on the red juice and, when crushed and processed, produce a red dye that doesn't fade. The dye is used extensively today in food and lipstick color.

For residents of such far-flung spots as Mexico, Sicily, Spain, Israel, Madagascar, and Ethiopia, the various parts of the prickly pear plant are still an important food. Practically all Mexicans enjoy prickly pear in some form, and for the poorer classes, it is an important part of their diet. Inhabitants of poor villages in parts of Ethiopia exist for three months of each year solely on prickly pear fruits. In Spain and Italy, the fruit is made into wine. Some Italian residents of New York City pay premium prices for imported prickly pears (also called barberry figs and Indian figs) for that all-important taste of home. Meanwhile, throughout the western United States, millions of tons of the fruit, far more than the rabbits and ground squirrels can eat, go to waste every year.

It is not only the magenta-colored fruits that are delicious. When properly prepared, the flattened stems or pads are a delicate vegetable. Mexicans on both sides of the border eat them in many dishes and chefs in upscale Mexican restaurants frequently have them on the menu. When they are used for food, they are called *nopales*, an Aztec word, or when cut into little pieces, *nopalitos*.

Prickly pear plants are in the genus *Opuntia* and range from small varieties that spread close to the ground and are covered with spines to tall tree-like varieties with few stickers on either the pads or the fruits. John Dicus, who operates Rivenrock Gardens in Nipomo, California, grows a variety he calls Nopal Grande that comes from the Yucatan Peninsula in Mexico where it has been cultivated for centuries. Nopal Grande pads are virtually stickerless and extremely tasty.

About 250 species of prickly pear are found worldwide, all of them originally from the Americas. They were taken to places like Europe, Australia, South Africa, and India as souvenirs by sailors and other early travelers. The first prickly pear plant arrived in Australia about 1839. It then spread rapidly and soon became a rangeland pest of gargantuan proportions. By 1886, New South Wales had passed the Prickly Pear Destruction Act and then followed with the Prickly Pear Destruction Commission. I have not located information that Australians ever eat prickly pear.

Health Aspects of Prickly Pear

NUTRITION

Both the fruits (Mexicans call the fruits *tunas*) and pads are low in calories because they are mostly water, with the fruits having about 85 percent water and the pads 90 percent. Each fruit provides about 12 calories. The pads contain about 37 calories per 100 grams, which is about two large pads.

The fruits are a good source of vitamins A and C with from 10 to 15 percent carbohydrates and 6 to 8 percent glucose and fructose. Nopales provide vitamins A and C, beta-carotene, and linoleic acid, which is an essential fatty acid. A one-cup serving of nopalitos provides 13 percent of the recommended daily allowance of vitamins A and C.

For generations prickly pear has been a folk remedy in Mexico and among Native Americans in the U.S. Southwest. As it spread across the globe, other cultures became aware of its benefits. The sap of the pads is similar to aloe and can soothe skin irritations such as burns, wounds, and sunburn. In Sicily the sap was used to reduce the itch of measles, in Sri Lanka and India it has been used on boils, and in China a split pad was bound on dog bites. Women in many cultures have found that pads that have been split and heated offer relief to breasts sore from nursing.

More recently, scientists, particularly several teams in Mexico, have conducted studies to test the real efficacy of the pads and fruits. The gummy quality in the pads, and to a lesser extent in the fruits, is caused by mucopolysaccharides—a fifty-dollar word that you can store away for use when you wish to sound authoritative. Traditionally, the pads were boiled and the sap rinsed away. It turns out that the sap is made up of substances that are extremely helpful in dealing with diabetes and high cholesterol. Researchers have found that eating cactus pads can help regulate blood glucose levels for those with non-insulin-dependent diabetes mellitus (NIDDM). An effective amount can be as little as 100 grams daily—two pads about the size of a small woman's outstretched hand.

The researchers noticed a significant benefit in just two hours after the meals and more improvement after four and six hours. Partially this is a result of the high amount of dietary fiber, but something else is going on as well since prickly pear seems to increase sensitivity to insulin through some unexplained process.

Other studies have shown that prickly pear pads can reduce the blood levels of triglycerides and bad cholesterol while not affecting the level of good cholesterol. It doesn't matter how the pads are cooked, except the old method of boiling the pads and draining off the sticky juice, which just sends all the good gums down the drain.

Gathering Prickly Pear Fruit

Because prickly pear plants tend to alter their characteristics according to their environment and because they hybridize freely, it is often difficult even for experts to identify them as to species. For purposes of food gathering, it is not necessary to know the exact names of each plant, for all of them are edible.

The deep red fruits of the Engelmann's prickly pear (*Opuntia engelmannii*) are about the size of an egg and have the best flavor. If you have access to other varieties, just cut a fruit in half and taste the juice. If it is sweet and pleasant, then fill your bucket. If you are planning on making a recipe that requires the fruit in pieces rather than just the juice, look for the larger fruits because they are easier to peel and will give you more pulp for the time you spend in processing.

To pick the fruits, use tongs or heavy leather gloves. A bucket works best for gathering your harvest; the spines will stick through plastic or paper bags.

Prickly Pear Fruit Preparation

The following directions may appear complicated at first glance, but actually the processes are all quite simple. The only way to take advantage of this free-for-the-picking desert bounty is to invest a little time in preparing these fruits. Your effort will provide you with an unusual delicacy of brilliant color and lively flavor.

Four items are essential for working with prickly pears: tongs; good, fine tweezers; heavy rubber gloves; and a stiff vegetable brush. You are going to get stickers in your fingers so have the tweezers nearby, use them when you need them, and do not let the stickers become a big irritation, physically or psychologically. The late David Eppele, who ran Arizona Cactus and Succulent Research in Bisbee, suggested the best way to deal with many small spines in your hand is to coat the affected area with white glue. When it is thoroughly dry, peel it off. It works on the tiniest stickers, called glochids, better than tweezers.

Holding the fruits one by one with the tongs and wearing heavy rubber gloves, scrub the pears all over with a stiff vegetable brush, rinsing them frequently in a pan of water to dislodge as many stickers as possible.

To Make Prickly Pear Juice

Place as many prickly pears as you wish to process in a large saucepan, cover with water, bring to a boil, and simmer for about 5 minutes. Transfer the fruit to a blender container with a very small amount of water (about one-fourth cup) to get the process going and blend until the fruit is liquefied. Blend long enough to make sure the skins are pulverized to get all those nutrients in the juice. Place a strainer over a bowl and strain out the juice. If your strainer has a very fine mesh, that should do it. If your strainer has large holes, you'll need to line it with cheesecloth or muslin (a clean square of old sheet would work).

If you don't own a blender, dump the soft cooked tunas into the sieve and mash the fruits with a potato masher until all the juice has drained into the bowl.

Four cups of fruit, about one dozen, should yield 1 cup of juice.

To Make Prickly Pear Syrup

Combine 1 cup of prickly pear juice, the juice of one lemon, and 1½ cups of sugar in a small saucepan over medium heat. Slowly bring ingredients to a simmer. Cook until syrup begins to thicken.If you want a thicker syrup, stir in 1 teaspoon of cornstarch dissolved in a little cold water (adding dry cornstarch to hot liquid will result in lumps) and cook to thicken. Stir with a wire whisk if necessary to get a smooth consistency.

To Make Prickly Pear Fruit Pieces

Fill a medium-sized saucepan with water and bring to a boil over high heat. Plunge eight to ten washed pears into the boiling water and blanch for 10 to 20 seconds. Lift them out with a slotted spoon and transfer to a colander.

Spear each tuna with a long-tined cooking fork or hold with tongs and peel with a sharp knife. Don't wait for them to cool; the stickers are softer when they are hot. Slit each peeled fruit in half and carefully scoop out the seeds with a spoon, then cut the fruit into pieces. Prickly pears vary in size, but eight to ten pears will yield 1 cup of fruit pieces.

· · · · ·

If you are short of prickly pears, you can reserve the seeds and the pulp clinging to them in a bowl. Add a little water, and break up the clumps with your fingers. Let the mass soak for 30 minutes, drain off the juice, and discard the seeds. The juice can be used as a pleasant beverage, mixed with other juices, or concentrated by boiling down for use in the recipes.

Prickly Pear Citrus Marinade and Sauce

Prickly pear and citrus are flavors made for each other. This sauce is excellent on chicken or pork, raising either of these to company status. This makes enough for two large chicken breasts, two pork chops, or some boneless ribs. The recipe is easily doubled.   **MAKES ABOUT 1 CUP**

½ cup prickly pear syrup

½ cup orange juice

½ teaspoon minced or pressed
    fresh garlic

2 teaspoons lime juice

1 teaspoon Dijon mustard

1 teaspoon cornstarch

Combine all the ingredients except the cornstarch in a small bowl.

Arrange meat in a shallow dish and pour about ⅓ cup of the mixture over the meat as a marinade. Set aside the remaining marinade. (Alternatively, put both the meat and ⅓ cup of the marinade in a plastic storage bag.) Put the marinating meat in the refrigerator if you will be holding it for more than 30 minutes. You can marinate up to overnight.

When ready to cook, remove meat from marinade and cook on a grill or broil. Discard the used marinade.

Whisk the 1 teaspoon of cornstarch with the remaining ⅔ cup of fresh marinade and bring to a boil in a small saucepan. Simmer until thick.

Pour a little sauce over each piece of meat; pass the remainder.

Prickly Pear Salad Dressing

This goes great on all fruity salads. I especially like it on a bed of greens topped with diced pears and red grapes sprinkled with crumbled feta cheese and chopped walnuts. Add a few dried cranberries if you have them.   **MAKES ABOUT ⅔ CUP**

¼ cup walnut oil

¼ cup raspberry vinegar

2 tablespoons prickly pear
    syrup

1 tablespoon lime juice

Put the walnut oil in a small bowl. Whisk in the raspberry vinegar until the mixture has thickened. Stir in the prickly pear syrup and lime juice.

Prickly Pear Plum Ice Cream

MAKES ABOUT 3 PINTS

2 cups chopped mixed plums

2 cups washed prickly pear fruits

½ cup sugar

1 pint heavy cream or half-and-half

Place chopped plums in a small saucepan and barely cover with water. Simmer 5 to 7 minutes until tender; when done, remove from water.

Meanwhile, place prickly pear fruits in another saucepan, barely cover with water, and simmer until tender, 5 to 7 minutes. Transfer prickly pears to blender jar with just enough of the water to process. Blend, then strain through a fine strainer. Discard seeds. Check strained juice to ensure no stickers have gone through the strainer. You should have about 1 cup of prickly pear nectar. If there is more, return the nectar to the saucepan and reduce to 1 cup.

Combine the prickly pear nectar and simmered plums in a blender jar and blend for a few minutes. Strain to remove any plum skins. Return to saucepan, add sugar, and cook for a minute. Cool.

Whisk in the cream or half-and-half and freeze in an ice cream maker according to the manufacturer's directions.

Summer Jam

The middle of the summer brings wonderful peaches and plums as well as prickly pears. Combining them in this jam makes a brilliant garnet spread. Use at least 2 cups of plums for the pectin that is needed for the jam to set up. Choose any kind of plums — purple, red, or black — but use a few that aren't fully ripe. The lemon juice also contributes pectin and brightens the flavor. Chop the fruit into ½-inch to ¾-inch pieces. If instead of jam you'd like a fruit sauce for ice cream, pudding, or cake, just stop cooking the mixture before it has fully thickened.

Before you begin, read "About Jam" on page 11. MAKES 3 CUPS

4 cups chopped unpeeled
   peaches and plums

1 cup prickly pear juice

2 tablespoons lemon juice

3 cups sugar

Mix all ingredients in a heavy-bottomed pan. Bring to a boil, then adjust heat so the mixture barely simmers with small bubbles over about half the top. Cook for about 30 minutes. You don't need to hover, but stir occasionally to avoid sticking. After about 30 minutes, the mixture will begin to thicken and will need constant stirring in a figure-8 pattern.

Cook until the mixture is done according to the directions in "About Jam." Immediately ladle into hot, sterilized jars and cover.

Prickly Pear Blanc-Manger

The inspiration for this recipe comes from the New York Times food section, which adapted it from a Paris pastry shop. *The Larousse Gastronomique,* the bible of French cuisine, says that blanc-manger (pronounced blah-mahn-jhay) is one of the oldest sweets we know, possibly dating from Roman times. It is still very popular in France.

The original recipe called for raspberries, but it works wonderfully with prickly pear. It can be made in an 8-inch cake pan or, for a fancier presentation, in a 5-cup mold.   **SERVES 6**

1½ cups heavy whipping cream, chilled

¾ cup whole milk

3 tablespoons ground almonds

½ cup sugar

1 envelope (¼ ounce) Knox unflavored gelatin powder

½ teaspoon almond extract

2 teaspoons vanilla extract

1 cup small (¼ to ½ inch) prickly pear pieces

SAUCE

1 cup fresh or frozen mixed berries

¼ cup sugar

1 teaspoon cornstarch dissolved in 2 teaspoons water

Choose a medium bowl that holds 5 to 6 cups and a larger bowl that it will fit into. Fill the larger bowl with ice cubes and cold water. Set both bowls aside.

In a medium bowl, whip cream until it holds soft peaks. Refrigerate.

Bring milk, almonds, and sugar to a simmer over medium heat, stirring occasionally to make certain the sugar dissolves. While milk heats, put gelatin and 3 tablespoons of cold water in a microwave-safe bowl or small saucepan. When the gelatin is soft and spongy—after sitting for about 2 minutes—heat it in the microwave for 15 seconds. If using a saucepan, cook it over low heat to dissolve. Stir the gelatin into the hot milk mixture and remove pan from heat.

Pour the hot milk into the medium reserved bowl and set the bowl into the ice-water bath in the larger bowl. Stir in the almond extract and vanilla extract, stirring just until the mixture cools. You don't want the milk to gel in the bowl.

Retrieve the whipped cream from the refrigerator and gently fold it into the milk with a spatula, then fold in the prickly pear pieces. Spoon the mixture into the 8-inch cake pan or the 5-cup mold and refrigerate until set, about 2 hours. To make ahead, cover and refrigerate for up to a day.

TO MAKE THE SAUCE: Combine the 1 cup berries, ¼ cup sugar, and 1 teaspoon cornstarch dissolved in 2 teaspoons of water in a small saucepan over low heat. Stirring constantly, cook until slightly thickened. Cool to room temperature.

TO SERVE: Unmold the blanc-manger onto a serving plate. If it doesn't slip out of the pan or mold easily, wrap the bottom of the pan or mold in a kitchen towel soaked in very hot water. When it is unmolded, spoon the berry sauce over it and around the edges.

ABOUT JAM

The recipes here are just a way to get you started on inventing your own jams from desert ingredients. An Internet search for "jam" or "jam without pectin" will lead you to a large community of jam makers who are sharing their experiments and acquired wisdom.

The basic theory of making jam without added commercial pectin couldn't be simpler: Combine fruit and sugar and cook until thick. There are some refinements, of course.

Jam does need some pectin to gel so choose some high-pectin fruits such as apples, plums, or citrus. Under-ripe fruits also have more pectin so don't use all super-ripe pieces.

Use about the same amount of sugar as fruit or up to one-third less.

Choose a heavy-bottomed pan to cook your jam to lessen the chance of burning. The jam will take some time to cook—adjust the heat so that bubbles cover about half of the surface. At first, the mixture will be thin and will require only occasional stirring, but as it thickens, you should stir continually in that figure-8 pattern you learned in home-ec class. Use a long-handled wooden spoon to keep your hand as far as possible from the hot bubbling jam.

There are several ways to check whether your jam is finished. Once it has begun to thicken and is looking more jam-like than liquid, get a large metal spoon, scoop up some jam, then tilt the spoon for it to slide off. If it comes off in drips, it isn't done. If the drips combine to form a sheet, it is finished.

Alternatively, turn off the heat, put a spoonful of the jam on a saucer, put it in the freezer for a few minutes, and see if it is acceptably thick.

The most precise method is testing it with a candy thermometer. If you live at sea level, your jam is ready at 220 degrees F. For every thousand feet of elevation, subtract 2 degrees. Candy thermometers are not expensive and can help you obtain a more consistent product.

It takes some time for the jam to climb the last several degrees but keep a close watch on it—it can overcook very quickly and ruin the whole batch. Overcooking is actually worse than undercooking. If your jam is too runny, you can always pour it out of the jars and recook or use as a sauce. However, overcooked, gummy jam is stiff, unspreadable, and not tasty.

Once you've made jam several times you'll get a feel for when the jam begins to look done. Most important is to stir constantly in those last few minutes so it doesn't burn.

Brandied Prickly Pears

Make these in the fall and store them for the holidays. They make a wonderful addition to your own parties and are terrific for gifts. The recipe can be easily multiplied to suit your supply of prickly pears.

Since you will be using just the thin, fragile sliver of fruit flesh after removal of the skin and seeds, choose the largest fruits for this recipe so the slivers are unlikely to fall apart.

Follow the directions on page 7 for making prickly pear fruit pieces, but cut the pears into halves only. Try to preserve their shape as much as possible.　**MAKES 1 PINT**

1 cup apple juice

½ cup sugar

10 cloves

1 stick cinnamon

1 cup cleaned, peeled prickly
　pear halves

¼ cup brandy

Sterilize a pint jar and canning lid by boiling in water for 15 minutes.

Combine the apple juice, sugar, cloves, and cinnamon in a medium saucepan and boil for 5 minutes to form a syrup. Add the cleaned, peeled prickly pear halves and return to a boil over medium heat. Once a boil is reached, turn off the heat and remove the saucepan from the stove.

Place the fruit, syrup, and spices in the hot, sterilized pint jar leaving room on top for the brandy. Add brandy and screw on lid. Tip jar back and forth to distribute brandy in the liquid.

Store in the refrigerator for at least a week before eating to allow the flavors to mingle.

Prickly Pear Leather

Fruit leather is a good item to stick in your backpack for a no-fuss trailside snack.　**MAKES 1 ROLL**

2½ cups prickly pear fruit pieces
　(see page 7)

3 ounces frozen grape juice
　concentrate, thawed

2 tablespoons honey

Put the cleaned fruit pieces in a blender jar and whirl just until puréed. You don't want to liquefy them.

Mix the purée with the other ingredients in a medium bowl and spread on a large cookie sheet covered with plastic wrap. There should be a thin but very even coating. Cover with a screen or netting to protect from insects and set outside in the sun until dry but still pliable. Or you can dry the purée mixture in a food dehydrator spread on plastic-wrap-covered pans that will fit in the dehydrator.

When dry, carefully peel from the plastic wrap by forming the leather into a roll. This operation is more easily accomplished if the leather is warm. To eat, slice or tear off desired amount.

Dried Prickly Pear Pieces

Prepare prickly pear pieces (page 7).

Cover cookie sheets with plastic wrap and lay the prickly pear pieces on the wrap. Dry in the sun, protected from insects by a screen or netting, or in a food dehydrator. When the pieces are dry but pliable, carefully peel them off the plastic and store in a tightly covered container.

Enjoy them as a snack or use in the recipe for Dried Fruit Candy that follows.

Dried Fruit Candy

MAKES 20 PIECES

½ cup dried prickly pear pieces
½ cup dried chopped dates
½ cup golden raisins
¼ cup chopped walnuts
½ cup minus 1 tablespoon
    granola cereal

If fruits are not soft and fresh, soften them in a wire strainer set over (not in) a pot of simmering water for 5 minutes.

In a food grinder or a food processor using the steel blade, grind the prickly pear pieces, chopped dates, and raisins together (or chop fine with a heavy knife, rinsing it often to prevent sticking). Add the walnuts and ¼ cup of the granola and complete the grinding.

Whirl the remaining 3 tablespoons of granola in a blender until it is fine crumbs. Form the ground fruit into a long roll 1 inch in diameter. Spread the powdered granola on a flat surface and roll the fruit rope in it until the outside is thickly covered. Using a sharp knife, slice into 20 pieces.

In the unlikely event you will want to store this candy, do so in a tightly covered container.

Prickly Pear Sangria

You needn't use an expensive wine for this. Any good drinkable red or rosé will do. **MAKES 1 QUART**

2½ cups red or rosé wine

½ cup orange juice

½ cup apple juice

½ cup prickly pear syrup,
  commercial or homemade

½ apple, diced fine

½ orange, quartered and sliced

Combine the wine, juices, and prickly pear syrup and chill. Add the fresh fruit before serving from a bowl, or put a little fresh fruit in each glass.

Gathering Prickly Pear Pads

The most desirable varieties to gather for pads have the fewest stickers but you do not need a botany course to make that distinction. The large, virtually spineless variety developed by Luther Burbank and used as a landscaping plant is the most desirable. Some common names for this hybrid are Santa Rosa, Sonoma, California, Fresno, and Chico. The large Mexican variety is also easy to handle, but in the United States it does not grow in the wild. Other species have more spines and are more time consuming to prepare, but they taste fine.

To gather, use tongs to grasp the pad and a small knife to detach it from the plant.

All cactus pads should be picked when they're young and tender during the spring or in the summer rainy season. The wild variety is ready when it is about the size of a man's palm; the domestic varieties can get larger — about the full size of a hand. Mexican farmers who grow nopales commercially force new growth year-round by trimming their plants and fertilizing them. Older pads quickly develop a fibrous infrastructure and don't taste good.

Caution: In some states, it is against the law to pick the pads of prickly pears growing in the wild, although fruits anywhere and pads domesticated in someone's yard are legal. Check the laws in your state.

Grocery stores that cater to customers with a Hispanic heritage usually offer nopales in the produce department. You can sometimes find pads that have already been cleaned and diced.

Prickly Pear Pad Preparation

If you are using the Burbank spineless variety of cactus, you must still clean off the glochids — the little hairs that look so harmless but are really tiny barbs. To do that, place each pad on a flat surface and scrape off the stickers with a small, sharp knife, like a serrated steak knife. Put some muscle into it and scrape against the growth pattern from the tip to the base of the pad. Cut off the stem end, which is usually tough, and a one-sixteenth-inch strip around the entire edge of the pad. Rinse the pad and check closely under a strong light for remaining stickers.

Now the vegetable is ready for inclusion in dishes as varied as your imagination. Drying the pads or nopalitos (pads cut into pieces) slightly makes the sap nearly disappear while all the advantageous qualities remain. The gumminess can also be broken down by weak acids such as vinegar, lemon juice, and tomatoes and by heat.

You can dice the nopales into pieces ½ to ¾ inch square, toss with vegetable oil, and heat in a 375-degree oven for about 20 minutes. Or you can sauté them in a heavy frying pan. One of my favorite methods is to lightly oil the whole, cleaned pads and put them on a grill. Grill until the nopales have turned from bright green to a more olive color and are somewhat shriveled. At that point you can slice or dice the pads depending on how you will use them.

Nopalito Roll-ups

These roll-ups make a great hors d'oeuvre—any leftovers are good with a salad for lunch the next day. You need to use very fresh flour tortillas.   **MAKES ABOUT 64 PIECES**

1 cleaned prickly pear pad
   (see page 15)
4 green onions
½ green pepper
8 ounces cream cheese
2 tablespoons sour cream
2 to 3 tablespoons chopped
   green chiles
Shake of garlic powder
¼ teaspoon salt
¼ teaspoon freshly ground
   black pepper
8 8-inch flour tortillas

Mince prickly pear pad, onions, and green pepper using a knife or food processor. If using a food processor, be sure not to overprocess to a slush.

In a clean processor bowl, combine cream cheese (divided into 8 pieces), sour cream, green chiles, and seasonings. Process until mixed. Transfer to a bowl and stir in the vegetables.

If you are not using a food processor, soften the cream cheese in a bowl using the back of a spoon, then add the sour cream, green chiles, and seasonings and stir until blended. Stir in the vegetables.

Lay a fresh flour tortilla on a work surface. Spread some of the cream cheese mixture over the entire surface, getting to the very edges. Roll up as tightly as possible, then wrap in plastic wrap and refrigerate. Repeat with remaining tortillas. When the tortillas are cold and the cream cheese has firmed up, unwrap. Trim off the uneven ends and then slice into eight equal pieces.

The rolling process is something of an art—you may have to try a few before you get the hang of it. Don't be afraid to unroll, re-spread, and re-roll until you perfect your technique.

French Green Lentil Salad with Nopalitos

This is a great side dish to grilled chicken and is also a good vegetarian dish as it provides plenty of protein with the lentils and feta cheese. It's also an interesting potluck dish as it doesn't need to be kept hot, and it is unusual enough that nobody else is apt to bring the same thing. **MAKES 8 TO 10 SERVINGS**

15 black peppercorns

5 parsley sprigs

5 thyme sprigs

1 bay leaf

4 tablespoons olive oil, divided

1 medium carrot cut into
 ¼-inch dice

1 medium onion cut into
 ¼-inch dice

1 garlic clove, minced

4 cups vegetable stock or water

1¾ cups French green lentils

3 cups nopalitos (page 15) in
 ¼-inch dice

¾ cup diced red bell pepper

½ cup thinly sliced green onions

¼ to ½ cup crumbled feta cheese

DRESSING

⅓ cup hazelnut oil

3 tablespoons sherry vinegar

Juice of ½ lemon

Wrap the peppercorns, parsley, thyme, and bay leaf in a piece of cheese-cloth and tie with a string.

Heat 3 tablespoons of the olive oil in a large saucepan and sauté the diced carrot and onion and the minced garlic until soft. Add the bundle of herbs, the vegetable stock or water, and the green lentils and bring to a boil. Lower heat to a simmer and cook until lentils are tender, about an hour. Stir occasionally and add water if necessary.

While lentils are cooking, use the remaining 1 tablespoon of olive oil to apply a thin coating over the cooking surface of a large, heavy frying pan (a cast-iron skillet is good). Sauté the nopalitos in two batches, cook-ing until they have turned olive green and are looking a little shriveled and lightly browned. Set aside (they will have reduced to just 1½ cups).

Drain the lentils and transfer to a large, shallow bowl. Stir in the nopalitos, diced red bell pepper, and sliced green onions.

Pour the hazelnut oil, sherry vinegar, and lemon juice into a cup; whisk with a small whisk or a fork until thick and then pour the dress-ing over the salad and toss to mix. Sprinkle the top with the feta cheese. Serve warm or at room temperature.

Nopalito-Chorizo Flatbread

This makes a good brunch or a lunch with a salad. Cut into smaller squares to serve as a party dish or appetizer. If you own an electric bread maker, let it do the work of making the dough.

MAKES 8 LUNCH SERVINGS OR 24 APPETIZERS

1 package (¼ ounce) active
   dry yeast

2 tablespoons sugar

1¼ cups unbleached all-purpose
   flour

¾ cup warm water

½ cup whole wheat flour

¼ teaspoon freshly ground
   black pepper

½ teaspoon salt

½ teaspoon crushed coriander
   seeds

Vegetable oil for coating bowl
   and frying pan

1½ cups nopalitos (page 15)
   in ½-inch dice

¾ pound bulk chorizo

1 cup shredded Oaxaca,
   Manchego, or mozzarella
   cheese

In a bowl, mix the yeast, sugar, and ¼ cup of the all-purpose flour. Add ¼ cup warm water and stir. Let sit in a warm place until slightly foamy. Stir in the remaining all-purpose flour, the whole wheat flour, the remaining ½ cup of warm water, and the seasonings. Knead for about 5 minutes until the dough forms an elastic ball.

Put the dough in an oiled bowl, turning to coat the top, and let rise until doubled in bulk, about an hour.

Alternatively, put all of these ingredients in a bread maker and choose the "dough" setting.

While the dough is rising, lightly coat or spray a heavy frying pan with oil. Sauté the nopalitos over medium heat until they have turned olive green and are looking a bit shriveled and lightly browned. As the moisture evaporates the nopalitos will shrink to half the amount.

Set the sautéed nopalitos aside and brown the chorizo, breaking it into fine crumbles with a spatula. Drain on a double layer of paper towels to absorb the fat.

Heat oven to 450 degrees. When dough has risen, punch it down and pat into a greased 9- by 12-inch pan. Evenly sprinkle the cooked chorizo over the dough, then top with the nopalitos, evenly spaced. Finish with the cheese.

Bake for about 12 minutes. Cut into 8 lunch or 24 appetizer squares.

Nopalitos con Crema

Joanne Stuhr is a noted art consultant—she can help you sell your collection or mount an exhibit. This delicious pale green dish, which she served as part of a Mexican buffet, is an art creation in itself. Use prepared nopalitos or fix them yourself from fresh pads (page 15). Make it easier by buying the chiles already roasted or prepare them beforehand as time permits and store them for a day or two in the refrigerator.

Crema Mexicana is a cultured milk product available in the dairy case in Hispanic markets. You can substitute sour cream thinned with milk or cream and add a pinch of salt.   MAKES 6 TO 8 SERVINGS

1 small onion

2 cloves garlic

2 to 3 tablespoons olive oil

2 cups nopalitos, diced

1 cube or 1 teaspoon condensed
    chicken or vegetable broth

5 to 6 green chiles, roasted,
    seeded, and pulled into strips

⅔ cup crema Mexicana

Chop onion and garlic. In a frying pan, heat olive oil until very hot but not smoking. Brown onion and garlic.

Add nopalitos and sauté until onions are soft.

Add the condensed broth and chiles and stir to distribute. Add crema. Stir and heat gently.

Apple, Carrot, and Nopalito Salad

This is a Southwest twist on an old favorite with the dried nopalito bits substituting for raisins. But go ahead and add raisins, too, if you'd like. Golden raisins would be prettier.   MAKES 6 SERVINGS

2 cleaned prickly pear pads
    (page 15)

2 cups shredded carrot

1 cup shredded apple

DRESSING

½ cup mayonnaise

¼ cup milk (cow, nut, or soy)

1 teaspoon sugar

¼ teaspoon salt

Cut prickly pear pad into strips ¼ inch wide. Arrange on a cookie sheet or flat pan and dry in a low, 200-degree oven for 15 to 45 minutes, depending on how juicy your nopales are. Alternatively, put them out in the sun for a few hours, protected from insects by a screen or netting, until the strips are chewy, but not hard. Chop into small bits.

In a medium bowl, combine nopalitos with carrot and apple.

Make the dressing by combining the mayonnaise and milk in a small bowl. Season with the sugar and salt. Stir dressing into the vegetables.

Nopalitos and Chicken in Culichi Sauce

I love poblano chiles—they have a lovely chile flavor without much heat. If you'd like more zip in your sauce, add a jalapeño chile. You can make the sauce, taste, and then add the jalapeño if needed.

If you have a grill, cook the cactus pads (nopales) and the chicken at the same time. When you chop the nopales into smaller pieces, the result is called nopalitos.

This is good served over rice to absorb the delicious sauce. **MAKES 4 SERVINGS**

3 medium-size (hand-size) cleaned (page 15) prickly pear pads

3 poblano chiles

2 large chicken breasts

1 tablespoon vegetable oil

SAUCE

¾ cup chopped onion

2 cloves garlic, minced

½ cup half-and-half

1 teaspoon chicken base or powdered bouillon

½ teaspoon cumin

¼ cup tightly packed parsley leaves

1 small jalapeño (optional)

Cut the cleaned prickly pear pads into squares ½ to ¾ inches on a side. Set aside.

Sear the skin of the poblano chiles over a gas flame, on a grill, or under a broiler until lightly charred on all sides. Place in a plastic or paper bag or a covered bowl to sweat for a while, until the chiles have cooled and the skins have loosened, then remove skin, seeds, and stem and set aside.

Cut chicken breasts in ¾-inch dice and sauté in vegetable oil until done. Set aside.

Sauté the nopalitos until they're olive green, shriveled, and lightly browned.

For the culichi sauce, soften the onion and garlic in a little water until translucent.

In a blender jar, combine chiles, onion, garlic, half-and-half, chicken base or powdered bouillon, cumin, and parsley leaves and blend until smooth. Taste and blend in jalapeño if desired.

Combine chicken, nopalitos, and the culichi sauce and heat through.

Nopalito Slaw

MAKES 12 SERVINGS

2 cups cleaned (page 15) and
   sliced prickly pear pads
1 tablespoon olive oil
3 cups finely sliced green cabbage
1 cup finely sliced red cabbage

DRESSING
6 tablespoons extra virgin olive oil
3 tablespoons wine vinegar
1 teaspoon Dijon mustard
1 tablespoon honey

Slice cleaned prickly pear pads thinly, about the size of a French-cut green bean.

Heat oil in a heavy-bottomed frying pan over medium heat. Add prickly pear slices and stir until they change to a more olive color and are slightly shriveled.

Put the cabbage in a medium bowl, add the cooked prickly pear pads, and mix.

Prepare the dressing by pouring the olive oil into a bowl. Whisk in the vinegar and mustard until thick. Finally whisk in the honey. Pour over the vegetables, toss, and serve.

Saguaro

Unless you live directly on undeveloped Sonoran Desert land and have saguaros on your property, it takes some planning to gather saguaro fruits. They become ripe during the hottest part of the summer—late June to early July when the desert bakes most of the day under a white-hot sun and even the early mornings are hot.

When I go saguaro gathering, I get up about 4:30 a.m. Dressed in long pants and long-sleeved shirt, sturdy shoes, and a hat, I load the gear in my car at my midtown home and aim to be out among the saguaros just at dawn.

As the sky lightens in the east, I drive slowly along the mostly empty roads looking for short saguaros. The taller, older plants can reach to 50 or even 60 feet, so I'm looking for those 12 feet high or less, very short for a saguaro but about as high as I can reach with a pole. I park, gather my pole and bucket from the back of the car, and head for the closest saguaro, hoping to find something ripe. Getting the first splash of crimson in the bottom of the bucket is the real beginning of the day.

Gathering saguaro fruit does not entail a leisurely stroll from plant to plant—these cacti prefer to grow on steep, rocky hillsides. You need to clamber across ravines, pick your way up uneven slopes, and dodge other shrubs and plants. Occasionally, if there has been rain, you might be surprised by a few wildflowers.

As the sun rises, the heat builds rapidly. Alone with the plants, my only companions the doves and other birds looking for a saguaro fruit breakfast, I find myself talking to the saguaros. "So what have you got for me?" I'll ask. Maneuvering the rocky hills is strenuous, so when one plant contributes several fat, perfectly ripe fruits I am so grateful that I sometimes say thank you.

I might worry about my sanity, but I know others have felt the same way. The late desert chronicler Edward Abbey agreed, calling saguaros "planted people."

The desert Native Americans' respect for the giant saguaros is so great that they consider them nearly human. Gary Paul Nabhan, in his charming and insightful book *The Desert Smells Like Rain*, reports overhearing a conversation between an elderly Tohono O'odham woman and a boy from the city who wanted to know if one could ever collect fruits from the top of the saguaro cactus by throwing rocks to knock them off.

> "No!" Marquita replied with a strain of horror in her voice. "The saguaros—they are Indians too. You don't EVER throw ANYTHING at them. If you hit them in the head with rocks, you could kill them. You don't ever stick anything sharp into their skin either, or they will just dry up and die. You don't do anything to hurt them. They are Indians."

The saguaro harvest is the traditional beginning of the new year for the Tohono O'odham. They gathered as much fruit as they could to make into syrup or dry into cakes, but they also used a portion to make wine. The saguaro harvest coincided with the start of the summer rainy season. Called *nawai't* (to pull down the clouds), it involved invoking the intercession of a deity far away in a "rainhouse" full of wind, water, and seeds in the hopes of hastening the storms.

The various desert Indian tribes were usually fairly lean, but they could put on considerable weight while gorging on saguaro and organ pipe cactus fruit. Jacob Baegert, a colonial priest, reported during the eighteenth century that some Indians became so corpulent after eating huge quantities of the sugar-rich fruit that he was sometimes unable to recognize at first sight people he knew well. This is understandable when considering the nutritional punch in each fruit. Winifred Ross, in her 1941 University of Arizona master's thesis, calculated that each whole fruit contains about 34 calories and 2 tablespoons of dried saguaro seed have 74 calories. A serving of five fruits has 4 grams of protein and 5 grams of fat and is high in soluble fiber and vitamin C.

The saguaro cactus, being the most obvious plant in the desert, has become a symbol of the American West, particularly when it is positioned in front of a spectacularly colored setting sun. Actually, saguaros are hardly ubiquitous in the Southwest and in fact are much less common than other types of cactus, growing only in an area restricted to southern Arizona, small pockets in California near the Colorado River, and the northern part of the Mexican state of Sonora. Even within this area they rarely grow at elevations above 4,000 feet and are even finicky within that area. I once saw, in a Dallas airport shop, a mug emblazoned with "Texas" in gold script flanked by a saguaro, the closest of which was two states and around 800 miles away.

When the early professional botanists began categorizing desert plants, they originally placed the saguaro in the genus *Cereus* in 1848, but then two cactus-loving botanists named L. N. Britton and J. N. Rose decided that the plant was unique and needed a genus of its own. They named it *Carnegia gigantea* after the philanthropist Andrew Carnegie who had funded much of the research at the Desert Laboratory in Tucson.

In his exhaustive article on the saguaro, the late Frank Crosswhite wrote that some people believe that the real reason Carnegie was so honored was that it was hoped he would provide even more money:

> As the story is commonly told, Carnegie was asked to come to Arizona and look at the unusual plant which had been named for him. He obliged and was shown the great forests of saguaro near Tucson. . . . When told that these giants all now bore his name, he inquired innocently how such a characteristic and useful plant had evaded detection near a highly populated part of the state so long. When the blushing botanists tried to explain how it had been scientifically necessary to change the name of the plant and that the cactus had been well-known for many years, Carnegie reportedly became disgusted with a kind of science that could change well-established names of plants to cater to wealthy persons.

In the early years of the growth of the state of Arizona, many thousands of saguaros were thoughtlessly bulldozed to make way for homes whose yards then had to be replanted with something else.

In the last three or four decades there has been a growing awareness among Arizonans of the value and unique qualities of the big plants, and there are laws to protect them on publicly owned property. Reestablishing a saguaro forest is a very long process. Even after growing for five years, saguaros are only a few inches high; they do not flower until they are forty or fifty years old, at which time they are around eight to ten feet tall; and most of the best specimens — those with many arms — are probably about two hundred years old, many reaching fifty feet by this age.

Because of this, most homeowners today are proud of any saguaros on their property, build around them, and become quite dismayed if they show signs of damage.

Conversely, there are those few antisocial individuals who are so angry with the world that they attack saguaros as an ultimate statement of their hurt and disassociation from the rest of the community. If they are caught, they are punished, but that does not bring back the saguaros.

Gathering Saguaro Fruit

Starting sometime in May, depending on the temperatures that year, saguaros produce waxy white flowers, the state flower of Arizona, on the tips of the arms. By middle to late June, the fruits are becoming ripe and the outer husks of the fruits peel back, revealing a bright red inside that some people assume are the flowers. By the time the husks have broken open, the fruit inside has usually been eaten by birds. The perfect fruits to pick are plump but still closed, egg shaped, and showing just a little pink on the outside husk. The fruits on each plant ripen over a series of weeks, so you can revisit a plant several times.

The saguaro plant provides its own best gathering tools. A very long rib from a dead saguaro (or two ribs laced together) makes a strong, light pole that is perfect for reaching to the top of the taller plants. On the tip, affix a smaller crosspiece of rib with some wire. This you can use to hook the fruits or nudge them off the plant. You can also use a conventional citrus fruit picker, a long pole with a metal basket on the top. It has the advantage of hooking the fruit into the basket, but it only works on the shorter saguaros.

When you break off the dried flower at the top of the saguaro fruit, it will have a very sharp edge. This can sometimes be used to slit open the fruit. But you'll also need a small knife and a bucket or two to carry your fruit home.

Preparing the Saguaro Fruit Pulp

Once you get home with your harvest, cut open each fruit and extract the pulp into a bowl or large, deep pan. Saguaro fruits have very few stickers, but it is prudent to wear heavy rubber gloves while handling them. Use immediately in recipes or separate fruit, seeds, and juice for storage.

I like to break up the clumps and measure 1-cup amounts of the whole fruits into small plastic freezer bags. Flatten and store in the freezer. I bake very little during the hot summer months and this lets me store my harvest for later.

To Make Saguaro Juice or Syrup

Put your fruit pulp in a large bowl or a clean bucket if you have a lot. Add as much water as you have pulp. Plunge your hands in and break up the clumps as much as possible. Cover the pan with a clean towel and let it stand in a cool place while you wait 6 to 8 hours for the fruit to soak.

When the time is up, use a fine wire-mesh strainer lined with cheese-cloth to strain all the liquid into a large pot. Retain the seeds (see below).

TO MAKE CONCENTRATED JUICE OR SYRUP: Boil the liquid until it is re-duced by half for juice; reduce it further for syrup (see also syrup recipes below). Skim and discard the froth and impurities that rise during the boiling.

Preparing the Seeds

Spread the seeds remaining from the juice-preparing operation on a large, flat pan or tray and dry them in the sun, protected by netting from birds and insects. There will be some washed-out pulp on the seeds and this will dry whitish.

When the seeds are dry, break them up. Using a pan with sides at least two inches high or a bowl, vigorously shake the seeds; the white dried pulp will rise to the top and can be skimmed off until mostly smooth shiny seeds remain. Store the seeds in a can or jar with a tight-fitting lid.

· ·

The following two recipes are alternative ways to make saguaro syrup; see above for unsweetened, pure saguaro syrup.

Sweetened Saguaro Syrup

1 cup concentrated saguaro juice

½ cup sugar

½ teaspoon cornstarch

In a small saucepan combine saguaro juice and sugar. Whisk in the cornstarch. Bring to a simmer over medium heat and cook until sugar is dissolved and liquid is slightly thickened.

Saguaro-Pomegranate Syrup

1 cup concentrated saguaro juice

1 cup pomegranate juice

½ teaspoon cornstarch dissolved in 1 tablespoon water (optional)

Combine juices in small saucepan. Bring to a simmer and cook until reduced to 1 cup.

If you wish to thicken the syrup, whisk in the cornstarch and water. Cook, stirring, for a few minutes as it thickens.

. . . .

Here are recipes for saguaro sauces to accompany meat dishes and a cooling saguaro-juice sherbet.

Chicken with Saguaro-Merlot Sauce with Chipotle

MAKES 8 SERVINGS

3 cups merlot wine

2 cloves garlic

1 cup Sweetened Saguaro Syrup (page 27)

1 tablespoon chipotle powder

2 teaspoons lemon juice

4 cups 1-inch-square chunks of chicken-breast meat

2 tablespoons oil

Combine merlot and garlic in a small, heavy-bottomed saucepan. Simmer slowly until reduced to 1 cup. Add saguaro syrup, chipotle powder, and lemon juice.

Put the chicken-breast pieces in a bowl and pour in just enough of the sauce to coat the pieces. Stir until all pieces are covered. Reserve the remainder of the sauce. Allow to marinate in refrigerator for about 30 minutes. If any marinade has collected in the bottom of the bowl, remove chicken from marinade with slotted spoon and discard used marinade.

Heat oil in frying pan or wok. Add chicken pieces and sauté until cooked through. Heat remainder of unused sauce. When chicken is done, arrange on serving platter or plates and top with sauce. Pass any additional sauce.

Saguaro Barbecue Sauce with Ribs

If you are using pure saguaro juice, sweeten it with the honey. Saguaro syrup is sweet enough without the honey. MAKES 4 TO 6 SERVINGS

¾ cup concentrated saguaro juice (page 27) or ¾ cup Sweetened Saguaro Syrup (page 27)

¼ cup honey (if using saguaro juice)

¼ cup tomato sauce

1 tablespoon soy sauce

3 tablespoons lemon juice

¼ teaspoon garlic powder

½ teaspoon chipotle powder

½ teaspoon freshly ground black pepper

1 tablespoon brown sugar

2 green-onion tops, minced

6 to 8 pounds of spareribs

To make the marinade, combine in a bowl the saguaro juice and honey (or the saguaro syrup), tomato sauce, soy sauce, lemon juice, garlic powder, chipotle powder, black pepper, brown sugar, and minced green onion.

Place ribs in a large, sturdy Ziploc bag; add the marinade and securely zipper the bag shut. Place bag on a plate or in a pan and marinate in the refrigerator for 1 to 2 hours, turning several times.

When you are ready to cook, drain the ribs, reserving the marinade in a saucepan. Place ribs in a shallow pan, bone side down. Bake at 450 degrees for 30 minutes.

Meanwhile, bring reserved marinade to a boil and simmer for a few minutes, reducing until thick.

When ribs are done, drain off all fat. Pour reserved marinade over the ribs and reduce the oven temperature to 350 degrees. Continue baking another 15 minutes, basting frequently with the marinade at the bottom of the pan.

Saguaro Sherbet

This is a good recipe to use if you don't have an ice cream maker. You can make it in the freezer and get a good result. MAKES ABOUT 1 QUART

1 envelope (¼ ounce) Knox unflavored gelatin powder

1 cup concentrated saguaro juice (page 27)

½ cup boiling water

¼ cup sugar

1½ cups whole milk

1 cup heavy whipping cream

2 tablespoons lemon juice

In a mixing bowl, soften the gelatin in ¼ cup of the saguaro juice. Pour the boiling water over the gelatin and juice and stir until gelatin is dissolved. Add sugar and stir until dissolved, then add remaining ¾ cup of saguaro juice. Allow the mixture to cool to room temperature, then pour into a loaf pan. Freeze until it is partially set, around an hour.

At the same time, add the whole milk and whipping cream to a bowl and chill mixture in the bowl in refrigerator; also chill beaters to an electric mixer in refrigerator.

continues on following page

When juice mixture is thickened, transfer it to a deep bowl and beat with an electric mixer until frothy.

Beat the milk and cream in the chilled bowl until frothy.

Fold the two mixtures together gently until well combined. Add the lemon juice. Return to freezer and freeze until firm, 3 to 4 hours. At this point you may also freeze in an ice cream maker.

. . . .

The following recipes use saguaro fruit pulp, saguaro juice or syrup, and saguaro seeds, sometimes two together, sometimes each alone.

Quick Saguaro Bread

MAKES 1 LOAF

Unsalted butter or oil for
   greasing loaf pan
½ cup sugar
½ cup unsalted butter or
   vegetable oil
1 teaspoon vanilla extract
2 eggs
¼ teaspoon baking soda
¼ teaspoon cream of tartar
1½ cups unbleached all-purpose
   flour
¼ cup plain or berry-flavored
   low-fat yogurt
1 cup fresh or frozen saguaro
   fruit pulp (page 26)

Preheat oven to 350 degrees. Lightly grease a 5- by 9-inch loaf pan.

In a medium bowl, beat together sugar, butter or oil, and vanilla extract. Add eggs one at a time, beating well. Add baking soda and cream of tartar. Beat well. Add flour, yogurt, and saguaro fruit. Stir just until combined—don't overbeat.

Pour into prepared pan and bake in preheated oven for 45 to 50 minutes or until a toothpick inserted in the center comes out clean.

Creamy Saguaro Salad Dressing

This makes a good complement to fresh fruit or gelatin salads.   MAKES ABOUT 1¼ CUPS

½ cup heavy whipping cream
1 tablespoon saguaro seeds
1 tablespoon honey
1 tablespoon concentrated
  saguaro juice (page 27)
½ cup mayonnaise

Put whipping cream in a small, deep bowl; place it and beaters for electric mixer in refrigerator for about an hour (or a shorter time if you have room in your freezer).

Meanwhile, grind saguaro seeds in blender or coffee grinder. Set aside.

Remove cream from refrigerator or freezer and whip until soft peaks form.

In a small bowl, combine honey and saguaro juice; add mayonnaise and combine. Fold this mixture and the saguaro seeds into the whipped cream.

Easy Saguaro Ice Cream

This is handy to put together when you have just returned from a saguaro-gathering expedition and want to make something fast. Soften the ice cream by moving it into a bowl in large scoops. If you let it soften in the carton, the outside will melt while the inside stays frozen.   MAKES ABOUT 3 CUPS

1¾ cups slightly softened
  vanilla ice cream
1 cup fresh or frozen saguaro
  fruit pulp
2 tablespoons frozen orange
  juice concentrate
2 tablespoons triple sec (optional)

Combine all ingredients in a large bowl. Beat with an electric mixer or by hand. Pour into a loaf pan or return to ice cream carton and freeze until firm, about 2 hours.

Saguaro Fruit Lemon Cake

This is easy and delicious. The pink color of the saguaro usually disappears as it bakes. If you want it to stay pink, add a few drops of red food coloring.   **MAKES ONE 9- BY 13-INCH CAKE, ONE 8- OR 9-INCH ROUND TWO-LAYER CAKE, OR ONE BUNDT CAKE**

1 box (17 ounces) lemon cake mix

Zest of 1 lemon (reserve the
   lemon juice for the frosting)

1 package (3.4 ounces) lemon
   instant pudding mix

4 eggs

1 cup water

⅓ cup oil

1 cup fresh or frozen saguaro
   fruit pulp (page 26)

Red food coloring (optional)

FROSTING

3 cups powdered sugar

Juice of 1 lemon (reserved from
   cake ingredients)

Preheat oven to 350 degrees.

Grease and flour Bundt cake pan, 9- by 13-inch pan, or two 8- or 9-inch round cake pans.

Empty cake mix into a large bowl. Remove zest (yellow part) from lemon with zester or grater; add to cake mix. Juice the lemon into a small bowl and set aside.

Add pudding mix, eggs, water, and oil to cake mix and beat according to cake-mix package directions.

Make sure the saguaro fruit pulp is free of clumps. This may require squishing it around with your fingers. Stir saguaro fruit pulp into cake mix. If adding the red food coloring, add it now and stir. Pour batter into your prepared Bundt pan, rectangular pan, or round pans.

Place in preheated oven and bake for 40 to 43 minutes for the Bundt cake, 30 to 35 minutes for the rectangular cake, and 25 to 30 minutes for the round two-layer cake. Before removing from the oven check that a toothpick inserted into the center comes out clean. Cool cake and release from pan or pans.

TO MAKE THE FROSTING: Put the powdered sugar into a medium bowl. Add the reserved lemon juice little by little until frosting is desired consistency. Dribble over top of cake.

Saguaro Fruit Coffee Cake

MAKES 1 COFFEE CAKE

1 package (¼ ounce) active
   dry yeast

¼ cup warm water

1 teaspoon sugar

2½ cups unbleached all-purpose
   flour

3 tablespoons sugar

¼ teaspoon salt

2 tablespoons cold unsalted
   butter

¼ cup milk (cow, nut, or soy)

1 egg, slightly beaten

1 recipe Saguaro Seed Filling
   (see below)

Preheat oven to 350 degrees.

In a cup, sprinkle yeast over the warm water. Add 1 teaspoon sugar and stir until dissolved. Let stand 5 minutes.

Meanwhile, in a large bowl, combine flour with 3 tablespoons sugar and salt. Using two knives or a pastry blender, cut butter into flour until mixture resembles cornmeal. Add milk and egg and the yeast mixture to flour and mix well. Knead until dough is smooth on lightly floured board.

(If using a food processor, combine flour, sugar, and salt in work bowl. Add butter, cut into four pieces, and pulse. Add milk, egg, and yeast mixture and process until dough forms a smooth ball.)

Transfer dough to greased bowl, turning to coat all sides. Cover with a slightly damp towel and let rise in a warm place until doubled in bulk. While it is rising, make Saguaro Seed Filling.

When dough is ready, punch down and roll out on lightly floured board to a rectangle 10 by 16 inches. Spread with Saguaro Seed Filling. Using the long edge, roll up like a jellyroll; seal ends.

Place roll on greased cookie sheet; with a sharp knife, make several diagonal cuts in top, about ¼ inch deep. Let rise again until nearly doubled.

Bake in preheated oven for 30 to 40 minutes or until nicely browned. Slice when cool.

Saguaro Seed Filling

FILLS 1 COFFEE CAKE

1 cup fresh or frozen saguaro
   fruit pulp with seeds

⅔ cup raisins

1 cup apple juice

Dash of salt

1 teaspoon vanilla extract

1 teaspoon grated orange rind

Cook first four ingredients in small saucepan until most of the liquid has evaporated. Stir frequently to avoid scorching. Stir in vanilla extract and orange rind. Let cool.

Saguaro Breakfast Porridge

Serve this with your choice of milk and fruit for a delicious breakfast. Recipe may be expanded to serve as many as necessary.   **MAKES 1 SERVING**

¼ cup saguaro seeds
  (page 27)
¼ cup raw oatmeal flakes
1 cup water

Grind seeds and oatmeal flakes in coffee grinder or blender just until you have a coarse meal. Don't grind to a powder. Place in small saucepan with water and cook over low heat for 5 to 7 minutes.

Quick Saguaro Biscuits

MAKES 10 TO 12 BISCUITS

¼ cup saguaro seeds (page 27),
  for grinding
2 cups biscuit mix
½ cup plus 2 tablespoons cold
  water
½ cup shredded cheese of choice
1 egg
1 tablespoon whole saguaro
  seeds, for sprinkling biscuit
  tops

Preheat oven to 450 degrees. Oil pan or cookie sheet.

Grind the ¼ cup of saguaro seeds in a blender or coffee grinder. In a medium bowl, combine ground seeds, biscuit mix, ½ cup plus 1 table-spoon cold water, and shredded cheese. Stir with a fork to form a soft dough. Pat dough into a ball on a floured surfaced and knead five times.

Roll dough ¼ inch thick and cut with a juice glass or a biscuit cutter. Arrange biscuits with sides touching in the pan or on the cookie sheet.

In a small bowl, beat egg and the remaining 1 tablespoon of water. Brush tops of biscuits with the egg mixture. Sprinkle the remaining 1 tablespoon of whole saguaro seeds over the biscuits.

Bake in preheated oven for 8 to 10 minutes. Serve warm.

Saguaro Pilaf

MAKES 4 SERVINGS

½ cup saguaro seeds (page 27)

1 cup bulgur

¼ cup chopped raisins (optional)

2 tablespoons sunflower seeds
   (optional)

1½ cups boiling water

3 or 4 green onions

1 to 2 tablespoons olive oil

Salt and freshly ground black
   pepper to taste

Grind saguaro seeds in blender or coffee grinder. Combine seeds and bulgur with chopped raisins and sunflower seeds (if desired) in a heavy saucepan with a lid. Add the boiling water. Cover and let sit for 30 minutes.

Chop green onions and sauté in the oil.

When 30 minutes is up, check to see if all water has been absorbed by the bulgur mixture. If not, cook and toss with a fork over low heat for a few minutes until water is absorbed.

Add green onions, salt and pepper to taste, and toss to combine.

Black Beauty Wafers

MAKES 16 WAFERS

¼ cup saguaro seeds (page 27),
   for grinding

1 cup whole wheat flour

¼ teaspoon baking powder

¼ teaspoon salt

1 teaspoon sugar

¼ cup water

1 tablespoon cider vinegar

¼ cup vegetable oil

8 teaspoons whole saguaro seeds,
   plus more for sprinkling on top

Preheat oven to 400 degrees.

Grind the ¼ cup saguaro seeds in a blender or coffee grinder. In a large bowl, combine seeds, flour, baking powder, salt, and sugar. Add water, vinegar, and oil and mix, stirring and kneading until a stiff dough forms.

Shape dough into two rolls, 6 inches long and 1 inch in diameter. Then slice each roll into eight wafers.

For each wafer, sprinkle ½ teaspoon of whole seeds on a flat surface. Flatten the wafer and press into the seeds. Sprinkle more seeds on top.

Roll each wafer with a rolling pin as thin as you can manage—the thinner the crackers, the crisper they will be. Shapes will be irregular.

Transfer crackers to an ungreased cookie sheet. Bake in the preheated oven for 5 to 7 minutes. Watch closely to ensure they don't burn.

NOTE: If it is important to have consistent-sized crackers, use a sharp knife to trim the cut wafer dough into small rectangles, squares, or triangles. Gather the scraps and re-roll.

Saguaro Pie Crust

Quick-cooking oatmeal works best in this recipe because it is finer.

MAKES ONE 8-INCH PIE CRUST

½ cup saguaro seeds (page 27)
½ cup rolled oats
½ cup whole wheat flour
½ cup wheat germ
Pinch of salt
⅓ cup vegetable oil
1 tablespoon apple juice
 (approximate)

Preheat oven to 350 degrees.

Grind saguaro seeds in a coffee grinder or blender.

In a medium bowl combine ground seeds with rolled oats, flour, wheat germ, and salt. Add oil and toss until well blended. Moisten with apple juice until it binds together. (If you add too much liquid, the crust will not be flaky.)

Pat into an 8-inch pie pan. Bake crust in preheated oven for 10 minutes, until lightly browned.

Saguaro Crumb Crust

MAKES 1 PIE CRUST

Substitute ½ cup ground saguaro seeds for an equivalent amount of cookie or graham-cracker crumbs in your favorite recipe for crumb crust.

Saguaro Seed Kolache

Classically made with poppy seeds, the tender cookies are just a little fussy to prepare, but delicious when made with saguaro seeds. They are tasty but not overly sweet. **MAKES 40 COOKIES**

1¾ cups unbleached all-purpose flour

¼ cup ground almonds

¾ teaspoon baking powder

¼ cup sugar

Pinch of salt

½ cup unsalted butter

1 egg

1 teaspoon water

1 recipe Saguaro Seed Fruit Filling (see below)

Combine first five ingredients in a medium bowl. Cut in butter until mixture is crumbly.

Beat the egg and water in a small bowl, then add to flour mixture and stir until well combined. Knead lightly into a ball and refrigerate wrapped in plastic wrap to firm up dough while you grease two baking sheets and make the filling.

When dough is firm, heat oven to 350 degrees. Divide dough into fourths. Take out one section and leave the others wrapped in plastic in the refrigerator.

Roll dough out on floured board. Cut out 2-inch squares, using a ruler to square up the sections; gather scraps and re-roll.

Fill each cookie with a scant teaspoon of Saguaro Seed Fruit Filling point-to-point diagonally along the east-west axis. Bring the north and south points together over the top and pinch. Repeat with all the dough and filling.

Transfer filled dough with a spatula to greased cookie sheets and bake for about 10 minutes until lightly browned. Cool on paper or baking racks.

Saguaro Seed Fruit Filling

You can use any type of dried fruit—light or dark raisins, cranberries, dates, or apricots. If using soy or nut milk, start with ½ cup and reduce by gently simmering in a small saucepan until you have the required ¼ cup plus 2 teaspoons. **MAKES ENOUGH TO FILL 40 SAGUARO SEED KOLACHE COOKIES**

½ cup ground saguaro seeds

½ cup ground almonds

¼ cup plus 2 teaspoons evaporated milk or ½ cup soy or nut milk

¼ cup sugar

½ cup mixed dried fruit

In a small bowl combine ground saguaro seeds and ground almonds. Add evaporated milk (or reduced and cooled soy or nut milk) and sugar.

Finely chop the dried fruits. A little sugar sprinkled on them helps keep them from sticking to the knife.

Stir the fruit into the saguaro seed mixture. If the mixture is too wet, transfer to a small, heavy saucepan and cook for just a minute to dry out, stirring constantly to prevent scorching.

Cholla

Cholla-bud season is fleeting, but it comes at what for me is the most joyous and beautiful season, just as the desert is reawakening from its winter browns and grays. But you've got to get out and pick the buds while the petals are still tightly furled. Once the spring has warmed and the flower buds have opened, forming beautiful rosettes of every shade from yellow to orange to magenta, the cholla-gathering season is suspended until late summer or fall when the fruits have developed and begun to turn yellow.

The many forms of cholla—some delicate and thin as a pencil, others plump and sturdy—are distributed almost everywhere cacti grow, ranging from Canada in the north all the way to Patagonia on the very tip of South America.

It was a surprise to me when I learned that cholla and prickly pear are very closely related. They both belong to the genus *Opuntia*, the largest cactus genus. Its subgenus *Cylindropuntia* distinguishes the cholla species, with roundish cylindrical stem segments, from their close relatives the prickly pears, with flattened stem segments, which belong to the subgenus *Platyopuntia*.

All parts of all species of cholla are edible—the trick is to choose the tastiest parts of the most desirable types. The recipes given here are for the unopened flower buds and the fruits. The stem segments are edible also, but you would probably rely on them only if you were lost in the desert and starving, and then you would not be interested in recipes anyhow. Some species, like the pencil cholla (*Opuntia ramosissima*), have such small buds and fruits that they are not suitable for gathering.

To fill your basket with the choicest specimens, you need not memorize a long list of species names. On your gathering trips, simply look for the fattest buds and fruits with the fewest spines.

When it is time to gather cholla buds, the petals will be well formed, but still tightly furled. The portion attached to the petals should be quite plump. Use tongs to gather the buds and watch where you step, for the ground beneath cholla plants is always littered with broken stem segments.

Cholla buds are nutritious. According to Wendy Hodgson in *Food Plants of the Sonoran Desert*, a 100-gram serving (50 freshly baked buds) provides 1.4 milligrams of iron and 650 milligrams of calcium or 14 percent of the recommended iron allowance and 81 percent of the recommended calcium allowance for an adult male. Two tablespoons contains more calcium than a glass of milk with only 28 calories compared to between 100 and 150 calories from milk.

Cholla was an important food for Native Americans. Among the groups that used them were the Tohono O'odham, River Pima, Western Yavapai, and Apache. The buds and fruits were usually baked in a rock-lined pit.

Gathering and Preparing Cholla Buds

Use tongs to gather the cholla buds and place them one layer deep in a pan or basket. In historic photographs we see Tohono O'odham women gathering cholla buds in flat baskets. Was this because they knew that to pile them on top of each other in a deep basket—or a bag, as I used to do—would lead to the cholla buds transferring their spines to each other, making them more difficult to clean? The spines on a cholla bud grow out of small protuberances and are easily snapped off. But if a spine goes into one bud from another bud, it must be drawn out with tweezers.

Removing the Spines

Once you get your cholla buds home, the first step is to get rid of the spines. Before proceeding, find a good pair of tweezers, the best you can afford. (Don't skip this step.) Next, if you are processing only a few cholla buds, get two pans or bowls and fill one with clean, pea-sized gravel. Put a few of the buds in with the gravel and pour the contents back and forth from one pan or bowl to the other until most of the stickers are knocked off. Finish cleaning the buds with the tweezers.

The time-tested way to clean lots of buds is to use an old window screen that is still attached to its frame, or try nailing a piece of screening to a frame. Prop up each corner of the frame with a brick. Dump some of your harvest on the screen and roll the buds back and forth with a stick. The stickers will lodge in the holes in the screen and snap off. Finish the cleaning with tweezers.

This can be a time-consuming process. However, Linda McKittrick, wild-food enthusiast and sustainable rancher, has discovered a quicker way. Recalling how ranchers in Mexico and the Southwest burn the thorns from prickly pear pads so cattle can feed on the pads during times of drought, she thought she'd try that with the cholla buds. Spreading the buds on window screens or the wider-spaced screening called hardware cloth, she lights a propane torch and passes the flame over the buds. The stickers immediately glow and turn to ash. The process of cleaning a quart of cholla buds becomes minutes instead of hours.

If you are doing this activity in your yard or on your patio, do not forget to spread newspaper under the screen to catch the spines or you will be in agony the next time you walk outside in your bare feet.

Preparing the Buds

At this point the buds are ready to be rinsed and boiled or steamed for 20 to 30 minutes, until tender. Cooked buds can be added to stews or chilled and included in green salads or potato salad. The one drawback is that they are somewhat gummy.

I discovered how to deal with the gumminess by chance and sheer laziness. One afternoon the remains of a cholla-bud and squash luncheon dish sat for several hours in a skillet on my stove, slowly drying from the heat of the pilot light. When I finally faced the cleanup chore, the cholla buds were slightly shriveled. I idly popped one in my mouth and immediately realized that a miraculous transformation had occurred. The bud had acquired a wonderful chewy texture with no hint of the former gumminess.

Subsequent experimentation has shown that the buds can be quickly shriveled in a convection oven, in a regular oven turned on low, or in the sun. Just spread them out on a jellyroll pan. As they shrivel, any remaining stickers become very obvious, so look the buds over carefully and pick out anything you have missed.

If you wish to prepare cholla buds for long-term storage, they must be thoroughly dried after steaming. To prepare dried buds for eating after storage, soak them in water for at least three hours, then barely cover with water and simmer until tender. How long until tender? Here's the word from teacher and wild-food advocate Martha "Muffin" Burgess, who sells dried cholla buds and has been working with them for decades: "If they are well presoaked they may only take 25 minutes of simmering to tenderize, but it is entirely dependent on things we may not fully understand, like how early the buds were picked before the flower would open.

There is no standardization as to when the buds are picked."

Mary Paganelli, co-editor of the beautiful Tohono O'odham cookbook *From I'itoi's Garden,* suggests eliminating the presoaking and cooking for 30 minutes to an hour.

In all cases, after they are cooked, you might consider drying them just a bit if you find the gumminess unpleasant.

Here are some recipes using cholla buds.

Cholla-Bud Quiche

This is a great dish for brunch or a simple supper with a salad. If you are using eggs from your own hens or those from a farmers' market that are a little smaller than supermarket eggs, use four.

MAKES 6 SERVINGS

1 cup cleaned fresh cholla buds
   (pages 40–41)
3 large eggs
¾ cup evaporated milk or
   half-and-half
½ cup sour cream (light is okay)
4 to 5 green onions, sliced with
   some green
¼ cup chopped canned green
   chiles
½ teaspoon dried herb of
   your choice
¼ teaspoon each salt and freshly
   ground black pepper
1 9-inch pastry shell
1 cup grated Swiss or cheddar
   cheese

Preheat oven to 350 degrees.

Steam cholla buds in a steamer basket over boiling water for 15 minutes.

Meanwhile, in a medium bowl, whisk the eggs until frothy and lemon colored. Stir in the evaporated milk or half-and-half, and the sour cream. Then add the steamed cholla buds, green onions, green chiles, dried herb, and salt and pepper. Stir until well combined.

Pour into pastry shell. Top with grated cheese.

Bake for 35 minutes and check to see if custard is set. If still a little runny, bake for another 5 minutes or until set. Cool slightly to set before slicing.

French Bean and Cholla-Bud Salad
with Sherry Vinaigrette

Tonto Bar and Grill is known for its innovative southwestern fare. The charming dining room is located in the lodge on the site of the former Rancho Mañana Dude Ranch in Cave Creek, Arizona, just to the north of Phoenix. Current owners Eric Flatt and John Malcolm united to restore the building to its glory days while updating it for contemporary tastes and uses. Here is a recipe from chef Aaron Geister bringing cholla buds up to a new level. **MAKES 6 SERVINGS**

SHERRY VINAIGRETTE

1 cup extra virgin olive oil

2 tablespoons Dijon mustard

¼ cup sherry vinegar

3 sprigs fresh thyme, leaves
   removed and minced

SALAD

¾ cup cleaned fresh cholla
   buds (pages 40–41)

¾ pound green beans, cut into
   2-inch-long pieces

1½ tablespoons extra virgin
   olive oil

½ cup finely diced red onion

4 garlic cloves, sliced

1½ cups yellow or red teardrop
   (pear) tomatoes, cut in half

TO MAKE THE VINAIGRETTE: Put the olive oil in a small bowl. Stir in the mustard. With a small whisk or fork, whisk in the sherry vinegar. Stir in the thyme leaves and set aside.

TO PREPARE THE VEGETABLES: Steam the cholla buds in a steamer basket over boiling water until tender, about 15 minutes. Set aside to cool. Do this an hour or two ahead of time if you want the cholla buds to dry a bit.

Put the cut green beans in 2 to 3 quarts of boiling salted water and cook for 4 to 5 minutes until soft but still bright green. Drain and shock in cold water to prevent overcooking, then drain again.

Meanwhile, in a small frying pan, heat the 1½ tablespoons olive oil. Sauté the onion and garlic briefly until soft. Transfer to a medium bowl. Add the cut tomatoes, the green beans, and the cholla buds. Stir to combine. Add enough of the sherry vinaigrette to coat. Reserve remainder of vinaigrette for another use.

Heritage Cholla Salad

Father Eusebio Francisco Kino, a Jesuit missionary and explorer, brought wheat to Sonora and to what is now the southwestern United States in the late-seventeenth century. This was a great benefit to the native populations for it gave them something that would grow during the winter and provide a harvest in the spring when all their other food stores were depleted. Olives arrived shortly thereafter.

This salad brings together cholla buds with these other cultivated foods that have shared the land for centuries. Partially drying the cholla buds helps to reduce the gumminess. MAKES 4 TO 6 SERVINGS

½ cup cleaned fresh cholla buds
   (pages 40–41)
1 cup wheat berries
¼ cup chopped mixed olives
2 tablespoons olive oil
1 tablespoon red wine vinegar
   or lemon juice

Steam the cholla buds in a steamer basket over boiling water until tender, about 20 to 25 minutes. Drain and spread on a baking sheet in a warm spot to dry until they are slightly shriveled, from 1 to 2 hours.

Meanwhile, rinse the wheat berries, cover with water in a small saucepan, and simmer for about an hour until tender. Cool.

In a small bowl combine the cholla buds, cooked wheat berries, and chopped olives. Dress simply with olive oil and vinegar or lemon juice.

Cholla-Bud Primavera

To make an artful pasta primavera, the vegetables should be cut in a shape that reflects the shape of the pasta. You can't do anything about the cholla buds, cherry tomatoes, and olives, but the rest of the vegetables can be cut appropriately. Spaghetti or long noodles don't work as well as tubular shapes like penne. MAKES 4 SERVINGS

½ pound pasta
½ cup cleaned fresh cholla buds
   (pages 40–41)
½ cup zucchini pieces
½ cup yellow crookneck squash
   pieces
½ cup chopped red bell pepper
½ cup halved cherry tomatoes
½ cup green or black olives
½ cup vinaigrette dressing

Cook pasta in plenty of salted boiling water until tender. Drain, rinse, and set aside.

Steam the cholla buds in a steamer basket over boiling water until tender, about 20 to 25 minutes. Drain and spread on a baking sheet in a warm spot to dry until they are slightly shriveled, from 1 to 2 hours.

In a wok or large frying pan, sauté cholla buds, zucchini, yellow crookneck pieces, and red bell pepper.

Combine cooked pasta and vegetables in a bowl. Add tomatoes, olives, and dressing. Toss gently to distribute dressing.

Cholla-Bud Hash

MAKES 4 TO 6 SERVINGS

1 cup cleaned fresh cholla buds
   (pages 40–41)
2 medium zucchini
1 onion
1 tablespoon vegetable oil
½ to 1 cup cooked, shredded beef,
   pork, or chicken
Chile powder
Salt and freshly ground black
   pepper

Steam cholla buds in a steamer basket over boiling water for about 20 to 25 minutes. Drain and spread on a baking sheet in a warm spot to dry until they are slightly shriveled, from 1 to 2 hours.

Chop zucchini and onion and sauté in vegetable oil until soft. Add the cholla buds and the cooked shredded meat, season with chile powder and salt and pepper to taste, and warm through.

Cholla Buds and Tomatoes

MAKES 4 TO 6 SERVINGS

1 cup cleaned fresh cholla buds
   (pages 40–41)
1 16-ounce can chopped tomatoes
2 tablespoons unsalted butter
1 cup sliced onion
1 tablespoon unbleached all-
   purpose flour
1 teaspoon sugar
½ teaspoon salt
⅛ teaspoon freshly ground
   black pepper
Sprinkle of garlic powder

Steam cholla buds in a steamer basket over boiling water for about 20 to 25 minutes. Drain and spread on a baking sheet in a warm spot to dry until they are slightly shriveled, from 1 to 2 hours.

Empty tomatoes into a saucepan and chop into smallish chunks.

In a skillet, melt the butter and sauté the onion until tender but not brown. Stir in the flour. Add a little of the juice from the tomatoes and stir until you have a gravy.

Add the onions and gravy to the tomatoes in the saucepan along with the cholla buds and spices. Simmer 5 minutes to heat and blend flavors.

Cholla Fruits

Cholla fruits are available for several months in the late summer and fall and are usually used fresh. If you gather a variety that has abundant spines, clean according to the directions given for cholla buds (pages 40–41), then split in half, scoop out the seeds, and peel. Doing the tasks in this order shows you what a very thin shell of flesh the cholla fruit has and reminds you to make the peelings very thin.

Cholla Marmalade

MAKES ABOUT 1½ PINTS

1 cup ripe (yellow) cholla fruit,
    cleaned (page 46), seeded,
    and peeled
2 cups sugar
Juice of two oranges
1 tablespoon grated orange peel

Sterilize three half-pint jars and lids by boiling in water for 15 minutes.

Coarsely chop the cholla fruit in a blender or food processor.

In a heavy saucepan, combine the fruit, sugar, orange juice, and grated peel. Bring to a boil and turn down the heat so that the mixture just simmers. Simmer for about 30 minutes, stirring frequently until mixture is thick.

Pour into prepared jars and refrigerate or seal.

Chollate (Cholla Candy)

MAKES 24 PIECES OF CANDY

2 cups ripe (yellow) cholla fruit,
    cleaned (page 46), seeded,
    and peeled
1 cup golden raisins
1 tablespoon cinnamon
2 cups sugar
Juice of two oranges

Coarsely chop the cholla fruit and raisins in a blender or food processor (or use a wet knife). Combine with remaining ingredients in a heavy saucepan. Cook over medium heat, stirring often until mixture is very thick and able to hold its shape. Set aside until cool enough to handle.

Butter your hands and roll the cooled mixture into a long roll. Wrap the roll in plastic or waxed paper and chill. Remove plastic and slice into bite-sized candies.

Barrel Cactus

The scientific name *Ferocactus*, from "fierce," is certainly appropriate for these plants, for practically every species is covered with tough, sharp, sometimes hooked spines. It is a great adaptation for survival, for the flowers, the fruits, and even the flesh of barrel cactus are all edible.

The barrel cactus is also called *biznaga*. An early use involved cutting the flesh into strips and letting it dry slightly. Then it was boiled with saguaro syrup and dried. Later, Mexicans began making a candy from the flesh of the barrel cactus, cooking it in a sugar syrup. In some parts of northern Mexico and areas around Los Angeles, the barrel cactus has been overcollected for this purpose and is extremely rare. In the United States, there are laws against digging up cactus, although the regulations vary from state to state.

A better alternative is to use the fruits of the barrel cactus, which are spineless and have a smooth, waxy skin. The fruits set in the summer and are ripe when they're yellow. They are drier than saguaro and prickly pear fruit so can last past the summer on the plant. If you find ripe fruit on a barrel cactus much past the fall, be sure to check that insects haven't found the fruit first.

The fruits are easy to collect—just a twist will remove them from the plant. The skins are usually tender so a simple rinse will ready them for use. The fruit tastes light and lemony and the shiny black seeds are easily dislodged. The Indians who lived in what is now the San Diego area used the seeds as a kind of grain before the Spaniards arrived. The seeds can be dried, toasted slightly in a skillet over low heat, and ground in a blender or coffee grinder. Substitute them in any of the recipes for saguaro seed or add them to cereals. The seeds must be ground before use as their hard outer covering is a bit too sturdy for the human digestive system.

Barrel cactus fruits have the same slippery juice found in prickly pear pads. Although I'm not aware of any studies done on them, I assume the fruits contain similar gums and convey the same healthful benefits for controlling blood sugar as other desert plants with that property.

Finally, what about the myth of the barrel cactus providing a cool well of water for the lost traveler in the desert? A grain of truth, greatly enlarged by myth. To begin with, you need a machete to whack off the top of the barrel—your Swiss Army knife will not do. Once you have laid bare the interior of the cactus, you will not find a vat of clear water, but a soft pulp that must be pounded to release the liquid, which is often bitter.

Biologist Wendy Hodgson wrote in 2001 that "the taste varies from intolerable to barely tolerable." Since many of the early botanists exploring in the late 1800s and early 1900s wrote of Native Americans using the liquid, we must assume that the people were using only particular species. Drinking liquid from species with a lot of oxalic acid can lead to nausea or diarrhea, leaving a thirsty person worse off. You would do better to remember to take a canteen.

Many native tribes ate the peeled pulp of the cactus, the fruits, and even the flowers. Some groups separated out the seeds and ground them for bread or tortillas.

In the southwestern United States, most barrel cacti are from about one to four feet high, but there are some along the San Diego coast that are quite flat and ground hugging. Reports tell of barrels in the Imperial Desert in extreme southeastern California that tower to eight feet.

Barrel Cactus and Pineapple Cake

Barrel cactus fruits vary in size, some slender and some as big as a large hen's egg, so gather plenty and you can always use the leftovers another way. This cake is only about an inch high, but it is rich, so a small slice is satisfying. **MAKES ONE 9-INCH CAKE**

¾ cup sliced barrel cactus fruit
  (12 to 14 fruits)

¼ cup lightly ground barrel cactus
  seeds (from the fruit)

1 cup unbleached all-purpose flour

1 teaspoon double-acting baking
  powder

2 tablespoons sugar

2 tablespoons dry milk powder

½ teaspoon salt

3 tablespoons cold unsalted
  butter

1 egg

1 teaspoon vanilla extract

1 8-ounce can crushed pineapple
  in its own juice

½ cup sugar

1 teaspoon powdered ginger

1 teaspoon cinnamon

1½ tablespoons unsalted butter,
  melted

Preheat oven to 425 degrees. Grease a 9-inch springform pan with butter or oil and set aside.

To prepare the barrel cactus fruit, trim each end from the fruits (the blossom end is tough and extends about ½ inch into the fruit), then slice in half lengthwise. Scoop out the seeds with a spoon and deposit in a bowl. Slice the fruit into thin half moons. If you are doing this step ahead, you can spread the seeds to dry; otherwise, toast them in a heavy frying pan or wok. Lightly grind seeds in a blender or coffee grinder.

In a bowl, mix the flour, baking powder, 2 tablespoons sugar, dry milk powder, barrel cactus seeds, and salt. Cut in the cold butter as you would for biscuits or pie crust until you have coarse crumbs.

Crack the egg into a measuring cup and beat with a fork. Add the vanilla extract and enough juice from the canned pineapple to make ½ cup. Add this to the flour mixture and stir to make a stiff dough.

Turn the dough into the prepared springform pan and spread to the edges of the pan with your fingers or the back of a spoon. Place the barrel cactus fruit in concentric rings on top of the cake batter. Use the larger pieces on the edges and the smaller ones as you get toward the center. Top with ¼ cup of the crushed pineapple.

In a small bowl, mix the ½ cup sugar, ginger, cinnamon, and melted butter. Sprinkle over the top of the cake. Bake the cake about 25 minutes.

Barrel Cactus Coffee Cake

Use the recipe for Mesquite Apple Coffee Cake (page 84) and substitute barrel cactus fruits for the apples. Separate the seeds from the fruits, dry, lightly grind, and sprinkle over the top of the cake in place of the walnuts or pecans. Thanks to Johanna Stryker-Smit for this suggestion.

Barrel Cactus–Mango Salsa

This makes a good accompaniment to roast chicken or ham. The reason for toasting the cactus fruit is to dry up some of the gumminess. It is best to assemble the salsa right before serving or the cactus slices will reabsorb moisture and become gummy again. If you need to make it ahead, combine everything except the barrel cactus slices and stir them in just before serving.   MAKES ABOUT 1½ CUPS

½ cup barrel cactus fruit,
　quartered, seeded, and sliced
½ cup mango pieces,
　in ¼- to ½-inch dice
1 teaspoon finely minced jalapeño
1 tablespoon finely minced red
　onion
2 tablespoons slivered black olives
¼ cup roasted, peeled, diced
　poblano (or ¼ cup canned, diced
　Anaheim green chiles if you
　prefer)
½ cup lemon juice
2 tablespoons lime juice
1 tablespoon honey

In a dry frying pan, toss the cactus fruit slices until they are very lightly toasted and some of the moisture has dried out.

Transfer the cactus fruit slices to a medium bowl and combine with the mango pieces, jalapeño, onion, olives, and poblano or Anaheim chiles. Stir until combined.

In a cup or small bowl, combine the lemon juice, lime juice, and honey. Pour over the fruit and stir until combined.

Desert Sun Marmalade

This marmalade is a sunny yellow, just the color of a brilliant spring afternoon in the southwestern desert. The recipe is adapted from a citrus marmalade recipe in the 1964 edition of *Joy of Cooking*. Before beginning this recipe, read "About Jam," page 11. **YIELD VARIES; MAKES ABOUT 2 PINTS**

12 barrel cactus fruits

2 large lemons

5 cups sugar (approximately)

Sterilize four half-pint jars and lids in boiling water for 15 minutes.

Trim both ends from barrel cactus fruit. The blossom end is tough and extends about ½ inch into the fruit. Quarter the fruits lengthwise and scoop out all the seeds; cut fruit into slivers crosswise. Discard seeds or reserve for another use.

Cut the lemons in eighths lengthwise, then cut crosswise into thin slivers.

Measure the cactus and lemon fruit in a 4-cup measuring cup. Transfer the fruit to a large saucepan and add water equal to three times the amount of fruit; soak for 12 hours in the refrigerator, then simmer for about 20 minutes, cool, and refrigerate again for 12 hours. This will soften the fruit.

Divide the juice and fruit in half, into two bowls. Measure each quantity and add ¾ cup sugar for each cup of fruit and juice.

Cook one of the halves of juice, fruit, and sugar according to the directions in "About Jam" (page 11).

Ladle into sterilized jars and refrigerate or seal.

Cook and store the second batch the same way.

Barrel Cactus Chutney

Nice with Indian food or with any grilled meats or a vegetable dish that needs a little lift.

MAKES ABOUT 2 CUPS

12 barrel cactus fruits, seeded

2 tablespoons salt

2 teaspoons vinegar

2 cups water

1 cup chopped firm pear

½ cup golden raisins

2 tablespoons candied ginger, sliced or chopped

1 clove garlic

½ cup firmly packed brown sugar

½ cinnamon stick

¼ teaspoon allspice

⅛ teaspoon cloves

⅛ teaspoon nutmeg

1 tablespoon honey

Slice barrel cactus fruit into thin slivers to make 1 cup.

Make a solution of the salt, vinegar, and water. Soak the fruit for 1 hour in 1 cup of the solution. Drain and rinse; repeat the soaking with remaining solution; rinse again.

Combine the barrel cactus fruit and all the remaining ingredients in a heavy saucepan and cook slowly over low heat, stirring often until thick.

NOTE: Candied ginger can be found in the spice section of most grocery stores; however, it is more common and usually less expensive in Chinese groceries.

Crispy Barrel Cactus Seed Chips

Here's a nice use for the barrel cactus seeds left over from the other recipes.
MAKES 2 DOZEN CHIPS

1 tablespoon dried barrel cactus
   seeds, lightly ground in blender
   or coffee grinder
1 teaspoon yellow mustard seeds
1 teaspoon whole cumin seed
½ teaspoon freshly ground
   black pepper
¼ teaspoon coarse salt
Two 6-inch whole wheat pitas
2 tablespoons olive oil

Preheat oven to 350 degrees.

In a small bowl, combine the barrel cactus seeds, mustard seeds, cumin seeds, black pepper, and salt.

Carefully separate the pitas into two rounds each, then cut each into six wedges. Put them on a cookie sheet, rough side up. Brush them with the oil, then sprinkle on the seed mixture.

Bake until crisp and brown, about 7 minutes. Check frequently to make sure they do not burn. Cool.

Biznaga Preserves

This was developed by Dale Parra as a use for desert plants of Baja California. A lovely wine glass filled with these preserves accompanied her to many Mexican and international food conferences, where it always attracted much attention. MAKES 1 PINT

2 cups barrel cactus fruits

SYRUP
2 cups sugar
½ cup water
¼ cup honey

Sterilize one pint jar and lid or two half-pint jars and lids in boiling water for 15 minutes.

Slice both ends from each fruit and poke out the seeds; rinse fruit. Discard seeds or reserve for another use. Place fruit in a covered saucepan, cover with water, and simmer about 12 minutes.

Meanwhile, combine the syrup ingredients in another saucepan and simmer for 7 minutes.

Drain the fruits, add to the syrup, and cook over low heat, stirring occasionally, for another 10 minutes, taking care not to burn the mixture.

Pour into sterilized jars and refrigerate or seal.

Elderberries

Elderberry bushes and trees offer a lovely green lushness and shade to desert summers that tend to be brown and sun soaked. In European folklore, fairies and elves would appear if you sat underneath an elder bush on a midsummer night. The lovely elder possessed potent magic, with the ability to drive away witches and kill serpents. It is unclear whether this magic extends to critters more commonly found in the desert Southwest.

Elderberry trees were formerly more common in the West when the water table was higher. Now they are found mainly along washes or ditches or sometimes roadsides, where they get runoff from the pavement. The edible species is *Sambucus mexicana*, with blue-black berries. *Species with red berries are poisonous.* The bushes flower in the spring, between April and May, and the berries follow in the summer. Those at lower elevations bloom earlier and those higher up bloom later.

Elderberry flowers and the berries that follow grow in small sprays called cymes. The flowers are tasty and edible. The berries aren't very sweet, but have large amounts of potassium and beta-carotene, as well as sugar and fruit acids, calcium, phosphorus, and vitamin C.

Elderberries also have high levels of anthocyanins, powerful antioxidants that protect cells against free radicals while boosting the immune system at the same time. Elderberry syrup is marketed as a tonic to prevent flu.

When I first began experimenting with wild foods in the summer of 1970, I was thrilled to find lovely bunches of dark purple berries growing near my home. With friends who lived nearby, I gathered a big bucketful, crushed them, and we all drank a large glass of the delicious juice. We were thrilled to be "living off the land." A half hour later we were all in our bathrooms, dealing with the result. It was a good lesson—the prime lesson—for anyone interested in wild foods: Don't eat it unless you know something about it.

Apparently not everyone reacts so violently to raw elderberries, but please be cautious until you know in which camp you belong. The flowers seem to cause no digestive upset, and cooking the elderberries denatures the problem substances in the fruit. Do not eat any green parts of the elderberry, as these problem substances are abundant in green fruits, stems, and leaves, and are not removed by cooking.

When the flowers are used as food they are sometimes called elderblow. If you gather the whole blossom, it cannot develop into a berry. This is not a problem if you have access to lots of elderberry bushes, but it you have just one, and you want to use the flowers and berries from the same plant, shake the blossoms into a bucket just before they are ready to fall. The fruit-producing ovary will stay on the tree and grow into a juicy berry in a few weeks. Elderberries will stain clothing.

Elderblow Fritters

MAKES ABOUT 24 FRITTERS

1 cup unbleached all-purpose flour
1 teaspoon baking powder
Dash of salt
2 eggs, separated
½ cup orange juice
Oil for deep frying
24 elderblow sprays on stems
   or just the separated flowers
¼ cup powdered sugar

Combine the flour, baking powder, and salt.

Beat the egg yolks slightly and add the orange juice and yolks to the dry ingredients and mix.

Beat the egg whites until fluffy. Fold a little of the egg whites into the previously prepared batter to lighten it. Then fold in the remainder of the whites. If you are using the separated flowers, fold them in, too.

Heat the oil to 375 degrees. Drop the flower batter into the hot oil by tablespoonfuls and fry and turn until they are golden brown all over. Drain on paper towels. Sprinkle with powdered sugar.

If you are using the bunches of flowers, hold them by the stem end and dip them in the batter to coat them. Fry as above. Do not eat the stems.

Elderblow Tea

Here are several ideas for making tea from elderberry blossoms.

1. Cover elderberry blossoms with cold water and let them soak for a day. Strain out the blossoms. Add a squeeze of lemon and sweeten with honey to taste.

2. Since elderberry blossoms and sumac berries (see Lemonade Bush, page 173) appear around the same time, they can both be soaked together overnight, in proportions to your taste. Sweeten with honey.

3. Steep elderberry blossoms and sprigs of wild or domestic mint together in boiling water for 10 minutes. Strain. Good hot or cold over ice.

Elderflower Citrus Cake

This recipe is not appropriate for a day when you are rushing to get something together quickly. The double sifting takes time, but if you are ready to get out all your baking utensils and have a good time some spring day when the elderflowers are blooming, you can make a delicious light cake. For the grated citrus rind choose lemon, orange, or tangerine or a combination.

Do follow the directions exactly. You can bake the cake in two 8-inch round pans or a Bundt pan. Ice cake with a powdered-sugar frosting flavored with citrus rind and juice. Garnish with elderflowers.

MAKES ONE 8-INCH TWO-LAYER CAKE OR ONE BUNDT CAKE

2¼ cups sifted cake flour

1 teaspoon baking powder

½ teaspoon baking soda

½ teaspoon salt

5 tablespoons unsalted butter
    at room temperature

1 cup sugar

2 large eggs

1 teaspoon vanilla extract

1 tablespoon grated citrus rind

1 cup nonfat yogurt

½ cup elderflowers off the stems

Elderflowers for garnish

CITRUS FROSTING

3 cups powdered confectioner's
    sugar

1 tablespoon melted butter

1 tablespoon grated citrus rind

¼ cup citrus juice (orange, lemon,
    or tangerine)

Start by taking the butter out of the refrigerator so it can warm to room temperature. Grease and flour your cake pans and set aside. Preheat the oven to 350 degrees.

Sift the cake flour and measure 2¼ cups into a bowl. Add the baking powder, baking soda, and salt and sift all into another bowl. Set aside.

Put the butter into a medium-large bowl and beat on high speed until light. Add the cup of sugar and beat again until fluffy. Add the eggs one at a time, beating each in. Then beat in the vanilla extract and citrus rind.

Add the previously sifted dry ingredients in three parts, alternating with the yogurt, beginning and ending with the flour. Scrape the sides of the bowl with a rubber spatula to get everything mixed in evenly.

Transfer the cake batter to your chosen pans or pan. Bake the cake in the preheated oven for 40 minutes in a Bundt pan and about 25 to 30 minutes in the 8-inch pans. Before removing from the oven check that a toothpick inserted into the center comes out clean.

Loosen and turn the cake out onto a wire rack to cool, then ice with the citrus frosting.

TO MAKE CITRUS FROSTING: Sift powdered sugar if lumpy. Combine all ingredients in a medium bowl. Beat by hand or electric mixer until smooth and creamy.

If you want the icing stiffer, add a little more powdered sugar; if too stiff, try a few drops more of juice.

Two-Flower Ice Cream

Delicious is the word for this ice cream. Wild-food enthusiast and urban farmer Linda McKittrick had the idea to make the elderflower ice cream using flowers from her extensive garden. After her first experiment, which tasted very good, we talked about modifications and I added the lavender to my version.

It is light and refreshing. If you have your own lavender plants use just the buds; if not, be sure you buy dried lavender meant for culinary uses.   **MAKES ABOUT 1 QUART**

1 cup elderflowers removed
   from stems
1 teaspoon dried culinary
   lavender buds
3½ cups whole milk
½ cup heavy cream
½ cup sugar
2 eggs
1 teaspoon vanilla extract
Pinch of salt

Combine elderflowers and lavender in a saucepan with the milk and cream. Heat until just below a simmer then turn off the heat and let the flowers steep in the milk and cream for 30 minutes.

Place a mesh strainer over a bowl and strain milk mixture. Discard flowers. Return milk mixture to saucepan and add the sugar. Heat gently and stir to dissolve sugar. Turn off heat to cool a little.

In a bowl, beat the two eggs until lemon colored and frothy. Whisking steadily, add about ¼ cup of the hot milk mixture to the eggs. Continuing to whisk, add just a little more until you have added about half the milk and the egg mixture is fairly warm. Then you can add the warm egg and milk mixture back to the saucepan.

Stir in vanilla extract and salt. Turn the heat to medium and, stirring constantly, cook to form a custard. The mixture should look a little thick. If you use a candy thermometer, it should register 170 degrees. Remove mixture from heat and pour into a bowl. Cool a little bit and then refrigerate.

When cold, freeze in an ice cream maker according to manufacturer's directions.

OPTION: If you like a little texture in your ice cream, divide the milk and cream mixture and steep the lavender in one of the halves and the elderflowers in the other half. Strain out the lavender flowers and retain some or all of the elderflowers in the ice cream mixture.

Elderberry Syrup

Elderberry syrup is great on pancakes and waffles, on ice cream, and drizzled over a fruit salad. Don't wear your best clothes or even your favorite apron when making this—elderberries stain.

YIELD VARIES

2 quarts elderberries, washed

Sugar (amount depends on amount of juice you extract)

3 to 4 teaspoons cornstarch

3 to 4 tablespoons lemon juice

Sterilize two quart jars and two pint jars and lids by boiling in water for 15 minutes. Your yield will vary depending on how juicy your berries are so you won't fill all the jars.

Rinse the elderberries and pick over to remove any green or damaged fruit. Place elderberries in a nonreactive, nonaluminum saucepan and add just enough water to cover. Simmer gently for 15 to 20 minutes until soft. Mash fruit and strain juice through a jelly bag into a bowl. Alternatively, line a colander with cheesecloth or a clean, nonterrycloth dish towel and add the fruit; mash, then gather up the sides of the cloth and squeeze juice into a bowl.

Measure juice into the same saucepan. For each cup of juice, add 2 cups of sugar mixed with 1 teaspoon of cornstarch. A little lemon juice to taste will enliven the flavor. Stir to combine and cook over medium heat, stirring until the mixture thickens.

Pour into sterilized jars, cover with lids, and store in the refrigerator.

Elderberry Aperitif

A little elderberry syrup adds interest to inexpensive champagne or other sparking white wine. Just mix together the following: MAKES 1 SERVING

1 glass sparkling white wine

¼ teaspoon elderberry syrup (recipe above)

Elderberry Vinegar

Elderberry vinegar is wonderful combined with walnut or hazelnut oil for a dressing. Try it on a salad of spinach and strawberries. **MAKES ABOUT 1½ PINTS**

2 cups elderberries off the stem

White wine vinegar

Preheat oven to 300 degrees. Rinse the elderberries and pick over to remove any green or damaged fruit.

Place the elderberries in a nonreactive, nonaluminum ovenproof dish or pan. Cover with vinegar. Cook in preheated oven for 1½ hours, or until the berries burst. Remove from oven and let the mixture stand overnight.

Strain through a fine sieve lined with cheesecloth. Pour into sterilized jars and refrigerate.

Elderberry Pie

The labor here is picking the elderberries from all the little stems. Running the tines of a fork over the sprays helps. After you've got a bowlful, go over them again to remove even little bits of stems or green berries you missed the first time. Also, resist the urge to pop a few in your mouth during this process. Raw elderberries can be very toxic to many people. **MAKES ONE 9-INCH PIE**

Pie crust for 9-inch covered pie

3½ cups elderberries

1 cup sugar

2 tablespoons lemon juice

2 tablespoons cornstarch

4 teaspoons unsalted butter (optional)

Preheat oven to 425 degrees. Arrange the oven racks so one is in the middle with a rack below.

Roll out the pie crust dough and fit the bottom crust in the pie pan. Roll out the top crust, fold into quarters, and cover with a damp towel. Put both into the refrigerator.

In a nonreactive, nonaluminum medium saucepan combine elderberries, sugar, and lemon juice.

In a cup or small bowl, mix the cornstarch with just enough water to make it liquid. Stir into the elderberry mixture. Stirring very gently, bring to a simmer over medium heat and cook until thickened.

Pour into bottom crust. Dot with small bits of butter if using. Add top crust and crimp edges. Make a slash in the top crust.

Bake for 30 minutes. Reduce oven heat to 350 degrees. Put a cookie sheet on the lower rack to catch any spillover and bake until pie begins to bubble and crust is golden brown, about 20 to 25 minutes more. Cool pie on rack.

Elderberry Jelly

MAKES ABOUT FIVE 8-OUNCE JARS

3 pounds ripe elderberries

2 lemons

1 box (1.75 ounces) powdered
   fruit pectin (such as Sure-Jell)

4½ cups sugar

Sterilize jars and lids by boiling in water for 15 minutes.

Put fully ripe berries into a large nonreactive, nonaluminum sauce-pan and crush. Heat gently until juice starts to flow, then cover and simmer for 15 minutes.

Line a colander set over a bowl with several thicknesses of cheesecloth or a clean, nonterrycloth dish towel you don't mind getting stained. Pour in the berries and mash to release juice. When cool enough to handle, gather up the edges of the cloth and squeeze out remaining juice into bowl.

Measure 3 cups of juice and add to large saucepan. Reserve remaining juice for another use.

Squeeze lemons, measure ¼ cup juice, and add to elderberry juice. Mix powdered pectin with juice in saucepan.

Over high heat, quickly bring mixture to a hard boil, stirring occasionally. Immediately add sugar and stir in. Bring to a full rolling boil and boil hard 1 minute, stirring constantly. Remove from heat. Skim off foam. Pour immediately into sterile jars and seal with lids.

VARIATION: Use half elderberry juice and half apple juice and follow directions for apple jelly on the recipe sheet that comes with the commercial fruit pectin.

Nuts, Pods, and Seeds

Acorns

Balanophagy is a practice that is as western as Tombstone and much older than your great-great-grandfather. If you have not tried it you are missing out on a gastronomic treat. Actually, it is easier to do it than to say it, because "balanophagy" simply means acorn eating.

Acorns, the fruit of the oak tree, have been a popular food of humankind for thousands of years. It is probably safe to say that human beings have eaten millions more tons of acorns than they have of all the agriculturally produced grains combined. In earlier times, the Japanese, Persians, Sardinians, Spaniards, and Greeks all included acorns in their diets.

On our own continent, acorns were the dietary staple among the California Pacific Coast Indians. Anthropologists speculate that the reason California tribes did not develop agriculture is that by cultivating fields they would have had to work harder for less food than they were able to procure simply by harvesting nature's bounty of seafood and acorns. The Karok Indians of California explained the abundance of acorns in their homeland in a legend that tells of a man who took a long journey carrying only his pipe and a loaf of acorn bread. Whenever he stopped for a snack, he dropped crumbs, and acorns grew up.

Tribes in other parts of the West as well as the Southeast and woodlands of the Northwest also ate acorns, although they did not rely on them as heavily as did the Californians.

In earlier years, acorns were usually ground and made into mush or baked into a hard bread, but modern balanophagists need not be content with such plain fare. Properly processed, acorns can be included in a wide variety of dishes from stews to breads to pilafs.

Generally speaking, acorns compare favorably with grains in nutritive value, although they are lower in protein and higher in fats than either barley or wheat. They also have essential vitamins and minerals. Acorns, because of their slow rate of digestion, were one of the foods that protected early Native Americans from the diabetes that affects so many today. Acorn meal has only 8 percent starch digestibility compared to the 55 percent starch digestibility of white bread. It also has a very low glycemic index. The high fat content brings acorns in at 2,265 calories per pound compared to 1,497 calories per pound for wheat.

In the late 1970s, Grace Mitchell, then the chief of the Yavapai Apaches in Prescott, Arizona, told me that the cowboys in her tribe would take a pocketful of acorns with them as they rode the range and that would be their lunch. Acorn stew is a traditional Apache food that has persisted, particularly for special occasions, after other dishes have vanished. Basically, finely ground acorn meal is used to thicken the gravy of a beef stew.

As is true for virtually all wild foods, acorns have an unusual, earthy flavor, quite unlike anything you might find packaged in the grocery store. Taste buds vary widely among us humans; if you are susceptible to bitter flavors, you may find even the milder Emory acorns (bellotas) too bitter to be pleasant. The leaching process described below can rid the acorns of some of the tannin that causes the bitter flavor.

Persons who are accepting of new flavors find well-prepared acorn dishes very tasty. In the wild-foods seminars I teach, even my most skeptical students begin to show interest when they smell the rich aroma of baking acorn bread. The finished bread, cut while warm into thick, crumbly slices and spread with butter, is always devoured with scarcely a crumb left behind.

Bellotas are another food included in Slow Food USA's Ark of Taste, a compilation of delicious wild and cultivated foods disappearing from our collective larder. The Emory oaks themselves aren't gone, but the bellotas are not being collected and sold as they once were.

Picking and Processing

The first step is to locate an oak tree and secure a supply of acorns. They are ready to gather when the shells turn brown and they begin to drop from the tree, from late July in Arizona to autumn elsewhere.

The more than sixty species of acorn-bearing oaks in the United States can be classified into roughly three groups: white oaks, which produce crops of mild-tasting acorns each year; black oaks, which take two years to mature a crop of acorns that are usually quite bitter; and Emory oaks (*Quercus emoryi*), red oaks that also produce every other year. It is not necessary to be a botanist and know in which group a particular tree belongs; the taste test is sufficient to tell you which are the best acorns in your neighborhood.

Shelling is best accomplished by the old-fashioned smash-and-pick method. Gently crack the shells of the acorns with a hammer on a reasonably clean surface, then separate the meats from the shell. A tiny hole in an acorn shell means that a worm got to that nut before you did. Save your time and toss it out. About one cup of acorns in the shell will yield a half cup of shelled acorn meats.

After shelling, the next step is to process or leach the acorns to rid them of their tannin, a substance that is toxic in quantity and makes the acorns very bitter. The Emory oak grows in Texas, New Mexico, and Arizona and produces small acorns called bellotas so sweet that some people can eat them without leaching. Several other types, such as those produced by the white oaks (*Quercus alba*), are sweet enough so that a few eaten raw cause no ill effects. But most acorns must be leached using one of the methods described below, especially if you are planning on eating a lot of them.

Native Americans used to build a nest of twigs near a running stream and pour water over the meal until it was sweet, but this is very time consuming and most of us don't have a stream or creek in our backyards.

Gary Lincoff, who has taught wild-food-gathering classes in New York City for decades, taught me a method more convenient for the urban gatherer. Lincoff boils the nutmeats, changing the water every fifteen minutes or so as it becomes rust colored from the tannin. Acorns that are not terribly bitter will be ready after a half hour's boiling and one change of water. More bitter varieties may take up to two and a half hours and many changes of water. Lincoff suggests a double-pot spaghetti cooker for this operation, lifting the acorns with the inner strainer pot and discarding the tannin-filled water that remains in the outer pot.

The above method uses whole acorns. Leaching the acorns after grinding into meal exposes more surface area to the water. Since I am very susceptible to bitter flavors, I prefer to leach even the Emory acorns before using them. To leach the meal, I put it in a fine sieve or coffee filter and pour boiling water over it. Two leachings leave granules that preserve the wild acorn flavor but eliminate the bitterness.

This hot-water method dissolves some of the fat from the acorns. Native Americans who lived in the southeastern part of the United States used this boiling method as a means of extracting the acorn oil, which they then rubbed on their bodies. To these people the acorn was second only to hickory nuts as a source of oil.

The final step in all of the above processes is to dry the meal or nutmeats on trays in the sun, protected from insects, or in an oven heated to 100 to 150 degrees. Check the trays after an hour and if the nutmeats are still damp, stir them around and check again later. When the nuts are completely dry, grind in a food mill, blender, or grain grinder.

If you pass the resulting product through a sieve, you will be able to separate the very fine meal from the coarser chunks. The finer meal can be used like flour in the recipes below or incorporated into your own favorite recipes. The coarser bits can be treated like rice or grain in casseroles or used whenever a recipe calls for chopped nuts.

Acorn Gingerbread

MAKES ONE PAN 9 INCHES SQUARE

½ cup finely ground processed
   acorn meal (pages 68–70)
1½ cups unbleached all-purpose
   flour
½ cup plus 2 tablespoons whole
   wheat flour
1½ teaspoons baking soda
½ teaspoon salt
1 teaspoon cinnamon
1 teaspoon powdered ginger
½ cup molasses (dark or light)
½ cup honey
1 cup hot water
½ cup unsalted butter, softened
½ cup sugar
1 beaten egg

Preheat oven to 350 degrees. Grease a 9- by 9-inch pan.

Combine acorn meal, flours, baking soda, salt, cinnamon, and ginger in a bowl and set aside.

In another bowl, combine molasses, honey, and hot water and set aside.

In a large bowl, beat butter and sugar. Add egg and beat until combined.

Alternately add the sifted and liquid ingredients to the butter mixture until blended. Turn out into greased pan and bake about 1 hour, until a toothpick inserted in the center comes out clean.

Apache Acorn Stew

This is one of the old-time foods that Apaches still savor, especially for holidays and ceremonies.

MAKES 3 TO 4 SERVINGS

1 pound stewing beef
½ cup finely ground and
   processed acorn meal (pages
   68–70)
Salt and freshly ground black
   pepper

Chop beef into ¾-inch chunks. Place beef in a heavy, lidded saucepan and add water to cover. Add lid and simmer beef until it is very tender and is almost falling apart. Remove the beef from the broth and chop or shred the meat into very fine pieces. Return beef to broth.

Stir the acorn meal into the meat and broth and season with salt and pepper to taste. Heat the mixture and serve.

Bellota Cornbread

This recipe combines two Native American staples, acorns and cornmeal, and the earthy flavors complement each other.

If you find the bellotas too bitter for your taste and are going to leach the acorn meal, cut down some on the milk as the wet acorn meal will be providing some moisture. If you don't have buttermilk, sour 1 cup of milk with a ½ teaspoon of vinegar. **MAKES ONE PAN 8 INCHES SQUARE**

½ cup finely ground and
   processed acorn meal (pages
   68–70)

1 cup cornmeal

½ cup whole wheat flour

2 teaspoons baking soda

½ teaspoon salt

3 tablespoons vegetable oil

¼ cup honey

1 egg

1 cup buttermilk

Preheat oven to 350 degrees. Grease an 8- by 8-inch pan.

In a bowl, combine the acorn meal, cornmeal, flour, baking soda, and salt.

In another bowl combine oil, honey, egg, and buttermilk and add to the dry ingredients. Mix just until all dry ingredients are moistened.

Pour into the greased pan and bake for about 30 minutes or until a toothpick inserted in the center comes out clean.

Acorn Stuffing

Every few years in the weeks before Thanksgiving, I receive a phone call from an adventurous cook who tells me he or she is planning to prepare a wild-foods feast for their holiday guests. The caller usually asks my advice—what I'd suggest, where to get certain ingredients. I've never heard back from any of these callers as to the success of their venture. Surely it would depend on whether their guests had palates as adventurous as those of the cook.

If you've ever considered putting together such a dinner yourself, here's a recipe that would go well with turkey, definitely a New World bird enjoyed by early people throughout the Americas. It also goes well with chicken—just put the chicken pieces on top of the stuffing and bake the two together.

½ cup diced onion

½ cup chopped celery

2 tablespoons vegetable oil

3 cups crumbled Bellota
   Cornbread (see facing page)

½ teaspoon cumin

½ cup broth or water

Preheat oven to 350 degrees.

In a large frying pan, sauté the onion and celery in 1 tablespoon of the vegetable oil. Add the crumbled Bellota Cornbread, the cumin, and the broth and toss lightly.

Rub the inside of a quart baking dish with the remaining oil. Put the stuffing mix in the baking dish and bake for about 30 minutes.

Acorn Burgers

The late food authority James Beard was intrigued enough by this recipe developed by New York botanist Gary Lincoff to include it in his *New York Times* food column. **MAKES 2 PATTIES**

½ cup coarse-ground and
  processed acorn meal (pages
  68–70)

1 cup water

1 teaspoon salt

1 tablespoon unsalted butter

1 onion, finely chopped

1 egg

Salt and freshly ground black
  pepper

Vegetable oil for cooking

Combine acorn meal, water, and salt in a saucepan. Bring to a boil and simmer, covered, for 15 minutes, stirring occasionally.

Melt butter in a skillet. Add chopped onion and cook until soft.

Combine the onions, egg, and cooked acorn meal in a mixing bowl. Season to taste with salt and pepper and mix well.

Mold into two patties. Heat a little oil in a covered frying pan. Fry patties on both sides for about 5 minutes in the covered pan.

Acorn Burritos

This recipe is from Amalia (Molly) Ruiz Clark's book of family dishes called *Amalia's Special Mexican Dishes*. Molly was nearing retirement age when, at the urging of her children, she wrote this book. It has been very popular and led her to a new career as a teacher in a community college and at a cooking school. This recipe was from Molly's childhood in southern Arizona. **MAKES 2 BURRITOS**

2 small flour tortillas

1½ teaspoons unsalted butter,
  melted

⅓ cup firmly packed brown
  sugar

⅓ cup finely ground and
  processed acorns (pages 68–70)

Vegetable oil for frying

Brush the flour tortillas with melted butter and sprinkle on the brown sugar and ground acorns.

Roll up the tortillas, turning in the edges; fasten with toothpicks if desired.

Deep fry in hot oil until golden and drain on paper towels. Cut in half to serve.

Acorn Muffins

This recipe makes a rather dark, heavy muffin that is very good served with butter and honey or orange marmalade. **MAKES 12 MUFFINS**

½ cup finely ground and processed acorn meal (pages 68–70)

½ cup wheat bran

1 cup whole wheat flour

1¼ teaspoons baking soda

Sprinkle of salt

1 egg

3 tablespoons oil

¼ cup honey

1 cup buttermilk

Preheat oven to 400 degrees. Grease muffin cups.

Combine acorn meal, wheat bran, flour, baking soda, and salt in a medium bowl; mix well.

In another bowl, beat egg; add oil, honey, and buttermilk and combine.

Add wet ingredients to the dry mixture and stir lightly until just combined. Do not beat.

Evenly distribute into greased muffin cups and bake in the preheated oven for about 20 minutes, until a toothpick inserted in center comes out clean.

Instant Acorn Cookies

If you are planning a family camping trip near oaks during acorn season, pack the ingredients for these cookies, which require no oven, and send the kids out gathering. These easy-to-make cookies are just as good when prepared at home. **MAKES ABOUT 6 DOZEN**

1 cup processed acorns (pages 68–70) or fresh Emory acorns (bellotas)

3 cups quick oatmeal

1 cup flaked coconut

2 cups sugar

3 tablespoons cocoa or carob

½ cup milk (cow, nut, or soy)

½ cup unsalted butter

1 teaspoon vanilla extract

If using fresh, shelled acorns, boil for 30 minutes, changing the water midway through cooking. Drain.

Combine acorns, oatmeal, and coconut in a large bowl.

Bring remaining ingredients to a boil in a saucepan. As soon as the syrup boils, pour at once over the dry ingredients. Mix thoroughly with a spoon or your hands.

Drop on waxed paper and allow to dry briefly if you can wait!

Mesquite

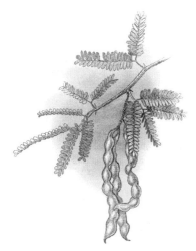

It is no wonder that Native Americans relied on mesquite pods as a food source for thousands of years. To begin with, their sweet taste makes them a perfect comfort food. They are abundant, easy to gather (no stickers), always available even in drought years, and nutritious with plenty of vitamins. And very important to a hunter-gatherer society, they provide sufficient calories per energy expended to gather them.

And yet, mesquite pods were almost forgotten as a food. In the late-twentieth century, health researchers seeking ways to address the growing diabetes problem among the desert Indian populations began to look at some traditional foods to see if the old ways of eating provided benefit. What the researchers discovered was that mesquite and some other desert foods, such as prickly pear, provided gums and fibers that the physiology of the native populations had become adapted to over many generations. Today we know that these desert plants are good for all of us, not just people with diabetes.

It is certainly easy enough to gather mesquite pods on your own. However, the growing interest in mesquite has led to opportunities for entrepreneurs to provide already ground flour for cooks who don't have the time or inclination to pick their own pods.

The Seri Indians, who live on the Gulf of California coast in the northern Mexican state of Sonora, are selling a delicious roasted mesquite meal.

Mark Moody, a young agriculturalist, began by harvesting and processing wild mesquite pods. He has now planted a nine-acre orchard of specially selected velvet mesquite trees in Arizona near the Colorado River.

Jeau Allen, at Skeleton Creek Farm in Aravaipa Canyon in southeastern Arizona, sells Moody's meal plus eight other varieties through farmers' markets and their website, and over in New Mexico, Al and Jane Smoake are supplying that market through their A & J Family Farms.

You can also find Moody's meal at farmers' markets in the Phoenix area, and he sells wholesale quantities through Arizona Mesquite Company.

Mesquite around the World

The southwestern United States isn't the only place to find mesquite trees. Various species of mesquite trees grow in arid places around the world.

Hawai'i seems an unlikely spot to find mesquite trees, but I found them growing in the dry areas of the southern part of the Big Island of Hawai'i.

When I was on a tour of the arid northwestern state of Rajasthan in India, I was amazed to see what appeared to be mesquite trees along the side of the road. At a rest stop, I left the group, dodged cars and trucks as I crossed the road, and ran into the nearby field to get a closer look. Yes, that was indeed mesquite. Later, I found out that it is the state tree of Rajasthan, where it is called *khejri* (*Prosopis cineraria*). The pods are eaten both green and ripe in curries and other preparations and the ripe pods and leaves are fed to animals. There is a popular saying there that death will not visit someone even in a time of famine if he has a khejri, a goat, and a camel.

Mesquite is also widely used in Peru, where the pods are collected and stored in large granaries. Much of the mesquite in Peru is processed into a molasses-like syrup called *algarrobina*, some of which also includes carob. I've included two recipes that use algarrobina. Mesquite meal imported from Peru, which has a lovely light flavor, is sometimes available commercially; however, shipping mesquite all that way when there are abundant pods in the Southwest seems to defeat the idea of eating locally.

Mesquite Nutrition

Because mesquite pods have the shape and size of a green bean, they are often called mesquite *beans*, which has caused some misunderstanding of how the fruit is used.

Not all of the mesquite pod is edible—a great deal of it is indigestible fiber. The most accessible edible portion of the pod is the pulp or pith between the brittle outside and the hard seeds. Ordinary bean pods do not have this pith. This pith portion has a very sweet, brown-sugary flavor and can be ground into a meal for use in baking. The pith surrounds a number of stone-hard seeds, inside of which are found the protein-rich embryos or true seeds.

TABLE 1. NUTRITIONAL ANALYSIS OF MESQUITE

Component	Whole Pod (100%)	Pith or Pulp (58% of Whole Pod)	Kernels or Seeds (13.9% of Whole Pod)
Crude protein	14.7%	10.5%	37.2%
Fat	3.2%	2.7%	6.3%
Ash	5.5%	6.4%	7.6%
Carbohydrates	46.3%	49.9%	32.1%
Sucrose	21.3%	21.3%	—
Inedible fiber	9.0%	13.4%	16.8%

Adapted from F. R. Del Valle, M. Escobedo, M. J. Muñoz, R. Ortega, and H. Bourges, "Chemical and Nutritional Studies on Mesquite Beans (*Prosopis juliaflora*)," *Journal of Food Science*, 48 (1983):914–919.

Mesquite meal is a good source of calcium, manganese, potassium, iron, and zinc. Although the protein content of the pithy part is low compared to common cereal grains such as barley, wheat, and rice, the seed is about 40 percent protein (see table 1), almost twice as high as most common legumes. Because it is relatively high in lysine, mesquite combines well with other grains that are usually low in this amino acid. Mesquite has no gluten.

The natural sweetness of mesquite is from galactomannan, a high-fiber gum. It turns out that this is great for people with diabetes because it has a low glycemic index. It takes mesquite longer to digest than many grains, thus maintaining a constant blood sugar level for a sustained time. It also reduces hunger longer between meals.

The trick to getting the most out of mesquite pods is accessing the protein of the true seed. It is almost impossible to crack the hard seed coats with home methods; however, in the past, Indians who lived in the desolate Pinacate Mountains on the Mexican-American border devised a stone implement given the name gyratory crusher by its discoverer, the late archaeologist Julian Hayden. It looks like a grinding stone with a hole through it, and for years investigators thought the artifacts they found were just worn-out grinding stones or metates. But Hayden surmised the hole had a purpose. As it turns out, when a heavy wooden pestle is manipulated in these stones, the mesquite seeds can be cracked, an ingenious bit of technology invented by protein-hungry people.

Luckily, today we have several alternatives to the gyratory crusher. One is a fairly common piece of farm and milling equipment called a hammermill. A hammermill can crush and grind both the pith and the seeds of mesquite pods and sift out most of the debris automatically. Mark Moody, the mesquite farmer in far western Arizona mentioned above, is producing meal with a ball mill that uses 150 pounds of steel balls to produce a fine product, which is then double-sifted. Moody maintains that the ball mill breaks up more of the true seeds of the mesquite, leading to a higher protein content of the meal, ranging from 18 to 21 percent, whereas other products are between 11 and 17 percent protein.

Gathering and Storing Mesquite

Mesquite pods should be picked when they are plump and golden. The flavor of the pods seems to vary from tree to tree, some being sweeter than others. The South American mesquites that have been used so widely as landscape trees produce plump, beautiful pods, but they do not have a good flavor. Better tasting are the pods from the native southwestern *Prosopis velutina*, also called velvet mesquite, and *Prosopis glandulosa*, or honey mesquite.

The major difficulty in storing mesquite pods is the tiny gray bruchid beetle. This is not an infestation that invades your harvest. The larvae of the beetles are already in the pods, the eggs having been laid as the pods were developing; the larvae eat the seeds and then burrow their way out. This was not perceived as a problem by the Indian groups who ate the odd insect part along with the mesquite and accepted it as inevitable. However, American desert dwellers do not eat insects these days. If you just gather the pods and put them away in a sack or can, you'll come back in a couple of months to have all your pods full of small holes and lots of tiny gray beetles. You can avoid this by microwaving the pods or freezing them until you can get them ground or use them in other ways.

Processing Mesquite Meal

The trick in processing mesquite is to extract the nutritious edible portion of the mesquite pod from the indigestible fiber. Grinding the dry pods by hand is laborious and difficult because the slightly gummy pith can clog up any grinding blades. The drier and colder they are, the better. Toast the pods in a 125-degree oven until they snap, then freeze them. Then you can break them into pieces and whiz the pieces in an electric blender or put them through a manual grain grinder. Sift out the seeds and husks through a fine sieve. Once you try this, you'll be encouraged to seek out a place to get your pods mechanically ground. The quality of the mesquite meal produced by a hammermill or ball mill is better because the mechanical milling breaks up the seeds, including much of their protein in the meal. Several ecologically based nonprofits offer this service for a small fee every fall in various parts of the Southwest.

Commercial Mesquite Products

The growth in interest in mesquite has led to the development and sale of commercial mesquite products. In addition to mesquite meal and jelly, another popular product is mesquite syrup, which is produced by Cheri's Desert Harvest in Tucson, Arizona; A & J Family Farms in Socorro, New Mexico; and others.

Algarrobina syrup, the molasses-like product imported from Peru, can sometimes be found online. Perhaps someday we'll see a similar product produced in the Southwest.

You'll find recipes for these products at the end of this chapter.

Mesquite-Banana Cake

I tend to be an improvisational cook—some of this, some of that, taste, correct. But this doesn't work for baking. All good cakes have a specific formula that has been carefully calibrated according to the way the ingredients perform with each other chemically and under heat. After my first attempts at a good, light mesquite layer cake were not satisfactory, I turned to the experts in *The Cake Bible*, by Rose Levy Beranbaum, and in *CookWise*, by Shirley O. Corriher, both of whom explain the process of devising a cake recipe—in detail. Cake flour, made from finely milled soft winter wheat, gives the best results. If necessary, you can use regular all-purpose flour, but save your unbleached flour and whole wheat flour for other uses.

As for the whipped cream frosting, the gelatin stabilizes the cream so it doesn't collapse and the cake can actually last for a couple of days in the refrigerator.

Cake is never going to be a health food, so follow the directions exactly and enjoy something delicious.

MAKES ONE 9-INCH LAYER

CAKE

1 cup ripe mashed banana
  (about 2 large)

¼ cup sour cream

2 large eggs

2 teaspoons grated lemon zest

2 teaspoons vanilla extract

1¾ cups sifted cake flour

½ cup plus 2 tablespoons fine
  mesquite meal

¾ cup sugar

1 teaspoon baking soda

¾ teaspoon baking powder

½ teaspoon salt

10 tablespoons unsalted butter,
  softened

FILLING AND FROSTING

1 teaspoon unflavored gelatin
  powder

4 teaspoons cold water

2¼ cups powdered sugar, divided

¼ cup cream cheese, softened

1 teaspoon vanilla extract, divided

1 cup whipping cream, divided

1 ripe banana

Preheat oven to 350 degrees. Grease the bottom of a 9-inch cake pan, line the bottom with parchment or waxed paper, then grease and flour the paper.

In a food processor process the banana and sour cream until smooth. Add the eggs, lemon zest, and vanilla extract and process briefly just to blend.

In a large mixing bowl, combine the dry ingredients and mix with an electric mixer on low speed for 30 seconds to blend. Add the butter and half the banana mixture. Mix on low speed until the dry ingredients are moistened. Increase to medium speed and beat for 1½ minutes to strengthen the cake's structure. Scrape down the sides. Gradually add the remaining banana mixture in two batches, beating for 20 seconds after each addition to incorporate the ingredients and develop the structure. Scrape down the sides.

Scrape the batter into the prepared pan and smooth the surface. Bake 30 to 40 minutes or until a toothpick inserted in the center comes out clean and the cake springs back when pressed lightly in the center.

Cool the cake in the pan on a rack for 10 minutes. Loosen the sides with a metal spatula and turn out onto a plate. Using another plate, turn right side up. Cool completely before frosting.

TO COMPLETE THE CAKE: Put a small, deep bowl and beaters into the refrigerator or freezer to chill. In a very small bowl or cup, dissolve the gelatin in the cold water. Set aside.

Using a long serrated knife, cut the cake longitudinally into two equal layers. Carefully transfer the top layer to another plate.

Heat the gelatin mixture for a few seconds in the microwave or in a saucepan until it completely dissolves. Stir to make sure it is completely dissolved. Let it cool while you do the next steps.

In a medium bowl, beat together 2 cups of the powdered sugar and the cream cheese. Continue beating while adding ½ teaspoon vanilla extract and 2 to 3 tablespoons whipping cream to make a smooth frosting. Spread on the bottom layer of the cake. Slice the banana and arrange the slices equally on the frosting. Add the top layer of the cake.

By this time the gelatin should be cool but still liquid. Pour the remaining whipping cream and the dissolved gelatin into the chilled bowl from the refrigerator and beat until soft peaks form. Sprinkle in 2 tablespoons of the remaining ¼ cup powdered sugar, beat, then add the rest. Add the remaining ½ teaspoon vanilla extract and beat until stiff. Frost the cake with the whipped cream.

Store the cake in the refrigerator until serving.

HIGH-ALTITUDE ADJUSTMENTS: Decrease baking powder by ⅛ teaspoon at 3,000 feet to 5,000 feet and by ¼ teaspoon at 7,000 feet. In this recipe, the bananas are your liquid, so decrease them by 2 tablespoons at 3,000 feet, 3 tablespoons at 5,000 feet, and up to ¼ cup at 7,000 feet.

Mesquite-Apple Coffee Cake

This recipe is built on a very popular Emeril Lagasse recipe. Emeril is always exhorting his television audience to "kick it up a notch," and the substitution of mesquite meal for some of the flour definitely kicks this cake up a notch or two.

Cut the apples into fine dice if you'd like them to blend into the cake, or a little larger if you like the apples to be prominent. Leaving the peels on provides vitamins and fiber.

For a fully desert creation, you can substitute barrel cactus fruit for the apples and replace the pecans in the topping with shiny black barrel cactus seeds lightly ground in a blender or coffee grinder.

MAKES ABOUT 18 SERVINGS

CAKE

2 teaspoons unsalted butter,
    for greasing
1½ cups unbleached all-purpose
    flour
1 teaspoon baking soda
1 teaspoon ground cinnamon
½ teaspoon salt
½ cup mesquite meal
½ cup unsalted butter
1 cup firmly packed brown sugar
2 large eggs
1 teaspoon vanilla extract
1 cup plain yogurt
2 cups chopped apples

CRUMBLE TOPPING

½ cup firmly packed brown sugar
½ cup unbleached all-purpose
    flour
¼ cup mesquite meal
½ teaspoon ground cinnamon
¼ cup unsalted butter, softened
½ cup chopped walnuts or pecans

BROWN SUGAR GLAZE

¼ cup firmly packed brown sugar
½ teaspoon vanilla extract
1 tablespoon water

Preheat oven to 350 degrees. Lightly grease a 9- by 13-inch glass baking dish with the 2 teaspoons of butter.

Sift together into a bowl the flour, baking soda, cinnamon, and salt. Stir in the mesquite meal and set aside.

In a large bowl, beat the ½ cup of butter and the sugar until light and fluffy. Add the eggs one at a time, beating after the addition of each.

Stir the vanilla extract into the yogurt.

Add the dry ingredients to the butter-sugar mixture, alternating with the yogurt. Stir in the chopped apples. Transfer to the prepared baking dish and spread to cover the bottom.

TO MAKE THE TOPPING: In a medium bowl, combine the sugar, flour, mesquite meal, cinnamon, and butter and mix until well combined. (This is easiest with your fingers.) Sprinkle the mixture over the cake and top with the chopped nuts. Bake until golden brown, about 30 minutes. Remove from the oven and cool.

TO MAKE THE GLAZE: When the cake is cool, make the glaze by combining the sugar, vanilla extract, and water in a small bowl. Mix until smooth, then drizzle over the cake. It will harden slightly after about a half hour.

Cut in squares to serve.

Mesquite Crisp Topping

With this topping you can turn any simple pan of sliced fruit into dessert.

You should have about a quart of sliced fruit. You want the butter soft enough to work but not quite melted. Depending on your taste, you could stir a few tablespoons of sugar into the fruit before adding the topping. Goes especially well with peaches or apples.   **ENOUGH FOR ONE PAN 8 INCHES SQUARE**

½ cup mesquite meal

1 cup raw oatmeal

⅓ cup firmly packed brown sugar

½ teaspoon cinnamon

4 to 6 tablespoons unsalted
   butter, softened

Preheat oven to 375 degrees.

In a small bowl, combine the mesquite meal, oatmeal, brown sugar, and cinnamon.

Add the butter in small bits and, with your fingers, distribute the butter throughout the other ingredients.

Sprinkle the mixture on top of a pan or shallow casserole of chopped fruit.

Bake in preheated oven for about 30 minutes.

Mesquite Crumb Crust

MAKES 1 PIE CRUST

Substitute ½ cup finely ground mesquite meal for ½ cup graham-cracker or cookie crumbs in your favorite crumb crust recipe.

Mesquite Log

This recipe produces an extravagantly delicious dessert. If you are artistic, you can frost it with chocolate frosting scored to look like mesquite bark. Decorate the plate with leafy mesquite twigs.

MAKES 8 TO 10 SERVINGS

TOPPING

¼ cup unsalted butter, melted

1 cup chopped pecans

1⅓ cups flaked or shredded
    coconut

1 can (14 ounces) sweetened
    condensed milk
    (not evaporated milk)

CAKE

3 eggs

1 cup sugar

⅓ cup mesquite meal

⅔ cup unbleached all-purpose
    flour

¼ teaspoon salt

¼ teaspoon baking soda

⅓ cup water

1 teaspoon vanilla extract

¼ cup powdered sugar

1 tablespoon cocoa or carob
    powder

Preheat oven to 375 degrees. Line an 11- by 17-inch jellyroll pan with foil.

In a small saucepan or a bowl in the microwave, melt the butter and spread evenly over the foil. Layer the rest of the topping ingredients on the butter and set aside.

In a blender, beat the eggs at high speed. Add the rest of the ingredients except powdered sugar and cocoa or carob and blend.

Pour evenly into pan and bake in preheated oven for 20 to 25 minutes. Since this is a very thin cake, watch carefully so the corners don't get overbaked.

Spread a clean, nonterrycloth dish towel on a flat surface and sprinkle with the powdered sugar and cocoa or carob. When cake is done, remove from oven and invert immediately on the towel. Carefully remove the foil. Starting with one of the long edges, roll the cake, using the dish towel to help. Cool. Frost or not. Slice to serve.

Holiday Bars

This recipe is good any time of the year, but is especially appropriate for Christmas. You can bake these bars in November when you have time and store them in tightly covered tins until the busy holidays. The candied fruit may be a commercial mixture or your own concoction of candied citrus peels, pineapple, dates, and raisins. MAKES 4 DOZEN BARS

1 cup honey
¼ cup water
3 tablespoons unsalted butter
2 cups whole wheat flour
1 cup mesquite meal
1 tablespoon baking powder
2 teaspoons cinnamon
¼ teaspoon cloves
½ teaspoon nutmeg
½ cup chopped walnuts
½ cup candied fruit

Preheat oven to 350 degrees. Lightly grease two 8-inch-square pans.

In a large saucepan, slowly heat honey, water, and butter until butter is melted and honey is liquid.

Mix flour, mesquite meal, baking powder, and spices in a medium bowl. Add to honey mixture and stir until well combined. Stir in walnuts and candied fruit.

Batter will be stiff. After dividing batter between pans, butter your fingers and pat mixture to spread evenly over pans.

Bake in preheated oven for 20 to 25 minutes or until a toothpick inserted into the center comes out clean. Overbaking will make the bars very hard. When properly baked, the bars will have a puffy look and a cakelike texture.

Remove from oven and cool in pans. Cut into bars when completely cool. To store, place in tightly covered tins.

Granola Blond Brownies

These bars require only one-fourth to one-third as much sugar as ordinary brownies, making them good for lunchboxes or snacks. MAKES 2 DOZEN BARS

1 cup mesquite meal
1 cup whole wheat flour
2 teaspoons baking powder
½ cup unsalted butter, softened
½ cup firmly packed brown sugar
2 eggs, beaten
1 teaspoon vanilla extract
1 cup granola (commercial or
    homemade)

Preheat oven to 350 degrees. Lightly grease a 9- by 13-inch baking pan.

In a small bowl, stir together mesquite meal, whole wheat flour, and baking powder. Set aside.

In a medium bowl, beat together butter and brown sugar. Add eggs, one at a time, beating in. Stir in vanilla extract. Stir in combined flour mixture. Stir in granola.

Bake in preheated oven for 20 to 25 minutes or until a toothpick inserted in the center comes out clean. When cool, cut into 24 bars.

Ginger-Mesquite Fruitcakes (Gluten Free)

Folks who are gluten intolerant are sometimes left out at holiday time. Not with these tasty little fruitcakes. All the sweetness comes from the fruit. If you don't like ginger, leave it out and substitute an equivalent amount of cinnamon.   **MAKES 24 MUFFIN-SIZE CAKES**

2 cups chopped dates (small
   pieces)
1¼ cups water
⅔ cup rice flour
½ cup tapioca flour
½ cup mesquite meal
1 tablespoon baking powder
½ cup ground almonds
2 teaspoons ground ginger
1 teaspoon apple pie spice or
   cinnamon
1 cup chopped dried apricots
½ cup chopped dried cranberries
½ cup chopped golden raisins
1 tablespoon grated fresh
   gingerroot
⅓ cup apple or apricot juice

Preheat oven to 325 degrees. Grease 24 muffin cups. Set aside.

Combine the dates and water in a small saucepan. Bring to a boil and simmer for a minute or two. Stir and cool.

In a medium bowl, combine the rice and tapioca flours, mesquite meal, baking powder, ground almonds, and dry spices. Stir in the chopped apricots, cranberries, and raisins. Stir in the cooled wet date mixture, the grated fresh gingerroot, and the fruit juice.

Divide the mixture among the 24 muffin cups. Bake for 20 to 25 minutes until bottoms of cakes are lightly browned. Remove from oven and remove cakes from cups to cool.

Turquoise Room Mesquite and Walnut Scone Pie

John Sharpe, chef and owner of the Turquoise Room in Winslow, Arizona, has gained a reputation for his inventive southwestern cuisine. His restaurant is located in the historic La Posada Hotel, built in 1929 to serve passengers on the Santa Fe Railway. Sharpe's inspiration for this dish came from the quince trees growing in front of the hotel. Planted in the 1930s, the trees are still doing well. Since quinces are hard to find, Sharpe wrote the recipe using apples in the fruit compote.

This recipe is from *La Posada's Turquoise Room Cookbook*, with seventy of Sharpe's other mouthwatering dishes. **MAKES 8 SCONES**

SCONES

½ cup unsalted butter, frozen

1½ cups cake flour

½ cup mesquite meal

¼ cup plus 2 tablespoons white sugar

½ tablespoon baking powder

½ teaspoon salt

Grated rind of half an orange

½ cup chopped walnuts

½ cup whipping cream

COMPOTE

4 to 5 good-size baking apples such as Granny Smiths or pippins

½ cup firmly packed brown sugar

2 tablespoons unsalted butter

1 tablespoon fresh lemon juice

¼ teaspoon powdered ginger

¼ teaspoon cinnamon

⅛ teaspoon ground cloves

1 pound fresh blackberries or blueberries

Ice cream of your choice

Preheat oven to 325 degrees. Lightly grease a cookie sheet.

The butter must be frozen, so before you begin preparing this recipe, cut it into ¼-inch dice and place in the freezer.

Place both flours, sugar, baking powder, and salt into a mixing bowl. Add the grated orange rind and walnuts to the flour and mix well.

Add the frozen butter and run electric mixer on slow until the butter is coated with the flour and broken down into very small pieces. You may also rub the mixture between your hands until the butter has mixed with the dry ingredients. Slowly add the cream and mix into a ball. Make sure the dough is sticking together, but be careful not to overmix the dough, which will make the scones tough—you want the butter flecked throughout in tiny pieces so the scones will be flaky.

Pat the scone dough out and cut it into 8 rounds with a biscuit cutter or a glass. (You can make smaller rounds and reserve the baked extras for another use.)

Bake on cookie sheet for 20 minutes or until lightly browned.

TO MAKE THE COMPOTE: Peel and slice the apples thinly. In a large saucepan over medium heat, combine the apples with all of the other ingredients, except the berries and ice cream.

Slowly bring the mixture to a low simmer and cook until the apples are tender. Add the berries and bring to a boil. Remove from heat and cool. Do not stir the mixture much, as you want the berries to retain their shape. Cover and refrigerate until serving.

When ready to serve, reheat the compote and divide into 8 shallow dishes. Place one scoop of the ice cream on top, and then top with a scone tipped to the side. If you have made the scones in advance, you can heat them in the microwave for 20 seconds, which will make them warm and crumbly.

Molly's Mesquite Tamales

Molly Beverly is food service director at Prescott College when she is not investigating wild foods and planning interesting ways to incorporate them into her café menu.

The mesquite meal sold by the Seri Indians (see page 77) is already toasted. If you are using your own mesquite meal, follow Beverly's directions on the next page for toasting.   MAKES 1 DOZEN

12 large corn husks or 24 small
   ones

Salt and freshly ground black
   pepper to taste

1 pound boneless free-range or
   backyard chicken thighs

1 cup cooked black or white tepary
   beans

4 ounces medium cheddar, grated

SAUCE

3 tablespoons vegetable oil

2 tablespoons New Mexico chile
   powder

½ teaspoon ground cumin

1 teaspoon dried Mexican oregano
   or epazote

1 teaspoon salt

1 tablespoon unbleached all-
   purpose flour

1 cup water

MASA

2 cups toasted mesquite meal
   (see note, next page)

2 cups fresh corn masa

½ cup unsalted butter, softened

¼ teaspoon salt

1 teaspoon baking powder

1 cup water or as needed

Preheat oven to 350 degrees.

Place cornhusks in a bowl and cover with warm water.

Salt and pepper chicken thighs. Place chicken on a baking sheet and bake for 15 to 20 minutes, until no longer pink in the middle. Let cool and then shred or cut into ½-inch chunks.

TO MAKE THE SAUCE: Heat vegetable oil in a small skillet over medium heat. Add chile powder, cumin, oregano or epazote, salt, and flour. Cook over medium heat, stirring constantly, until mixture sizzles and chile color deepens to a darker red. Add the cup of water, stir, and bring to a boil. Reduce heat and simmer until slightly thick. Taste and adjust seasoning.

Add chicken and beans to the sauce and let simmer for 5 minutes. Set aside.

TO ASSEMBLE THE MASA: Mix together mesquite meal, corn masa, butter, salt, baking powder, and enough water to make a wet but not runny dough.

TO ASSEMBLE THE TAMALES: Remove cornhusks from water and pat dry with a towel. Lay out one with the pointed end pointing away from you. Spread ¼ inch of masa over the cornhusk, leaving the top ⅓ uncovered. Now lay a vertical ribbon of sauce with chicken and beans on the masa. Cover with grated cheddar. Fold the right and then the left edge of the cornhusk over the filling. Finally, fold down the pointed end with one crease. Place your assembled tamale folded side down on a baking sheet. Repeat until all ingredients are used up.

TO COOK THE TAMALES: Place all tamales in a steamer. Put the folded end down and stand them up, so the open side is on the top. Steam over simmering water, tightly covered, for 45 minutes. Remove carefully and let sit a few minutes before serving.

NOTE: Raw mesquite meal can be toasted in a dry skillet. Stir constantly over medium heat until flour turns a light brown. Watch carefully as the meal will burn easily. Remove pan from heat and meal from pan immediately to stop the cooking.

Mesquite Ginger Cookies

MAKES 5½ DOZEN 2-INCH COOKIES

4-inch piece of fresh gingerroot

1 cup unsalted butter

½ cup firmly packed brown sugar

1 egg

¾ cup honey

1 cup unbleached all-purpose flour

1 cup whole wheat flour

1 cup mesquite meal

2 teaspoons baking powder

¼ teaspoon salt

Preheat oven to 325 degrees and lightly grease two cookie sheets.

Peel and grate gingerroot. Set aside.

Beat together butter, sugar, and egg until light and fluffy. Add honey and beat until combined. Add unbleached all-purpose and whole wheat flours, mesquite meal, baking powder, and salt and beat well. Take the grated ginger in your hand and squeeze the juice into the cookie batter; stir the juice in and discard the fiber.

Drop by teaspoonfuls onto greased cookie sheets. Dampen the end of a clean, nonterrycloth dish towel and wrap it around the bottom of a juice glass. Use this to flatten each dab of cookie dough.

Bake about 12 minutes until lightly browned around the edges. The cookies are soft and fragile when they come out of the oven, but they become firmer as they cool.

VARIATION: The brown sugar may be omitted with no noticeable change in flavor and only a slight change in texture.

Mesquite-Carrot Dinner Rolls

Fresh dinner rolls usually appear on holiday tables or for special feasts. These rolls are a way to introduce a little novelty to a same-old, same-old holiday dinner. **MAKES 12 ROLLS**

1 package (¼ ounce) active dry yeast

½ cup warm water

1 tablespoon sugar

1 cup grated carrot (about 1 large carrot)

1 cup warm milk (cow, nut, or soy)

1 tablespoon unsalted butter, softened, plus a teaspoon for bowl

1 teaspoon salt

2 to 2½ cups unbleached all-purpose flour plus more for kneading

½ cup whole wheat flour

½ cup mesquite meal

In a large bowl, dissolve yeast in the ½ cup of warm water and add the sugar. Let stand for about 15 minutes until frothy.

While that is going on, grate the carrot and assemble the remaining ingredients.

Add the milk, butter, and salt to the yeast and sugar mixture and stir to combine. Add ½ cup of the all-purpose flour and the whole wheat flour and beat for about a minute with a large spoon to develop the gluten. Add mesquite meal and beat again. Add grated carrot and remaining 1½ to 2 cups of all-purpose flour in ½-cup increments (dough should just hold together) and stir until combined.

Turn out onto a floured board and knead for about 5 minutes until you have an elastic ball, adding more flour as necessary to prevent sticking.

Grease a large bowl with the teaspoon of butter. Add the dough, turning to coat. Cover with a clean, nonterrycloth dish towel and place in a warm place to rise. When dough has doubled in bulk, make a fist and punch it down.

Preheat oven to 425 degrees. Remove dough from bowl and knead a few turns. Divide dough into 12 pieces and fashion plump, smooth rolls.

Place rolls in greased 8-inch round pan or 8-inch-square pan, cover with the towel, and allow to rise again until doubled. Bake for 15 to 20 minutes or until lightly browned.

Mesquite Hotcakes

These hotcakes can be made vegan with egg substitute (such as Ener-G egg replacer) and organic, unsweetened soymilk or nut milk instead of dairy milk.

Desert Harvesters serves hundreds of mesquite pancakes every autumn in Tucson when they invite people to bring their mesquite pods for mechanical grinding. There are as many good hotcake recipes as there are cooks; here's one to try. *Eat Mesquite!*, the Desert Harvesters' mesquite cookbook, has two other recipes. Try them all — or invent your own — and discover your favorite. **MAKES TWENTY 4-INCH HOTCAKES**

1½ cups unbleached all-purpose flour

3 tablespoons sugar

½ teaspoon salt

1 tablespoon baking powder

2 eggs

7 tablespoons oil

2 cups milk

½ cup mesquite meal

Sift together into a bowl the flour, sugar, salt, and baking powder. Set aside.

In a large bowl, beat together eggs, oil, and milk. Stir in mesquite meal, then stir in flour mixture (batter will be lumpy). Add a little more milk if you wish to have a thinner batter.

Cook on heated grill until bubbles form on the top. Turn and cook until reverse side is browned.

Mesquite Crackers

Because these crackers are easy to pack and ship, they have traveled to several international conferences dealing with mesquite. We also served them topped with goat cheese at a dinner simulating food that might have been eaten by early settlers in the Presidio San Agustín del Tucson, founded in 1775.
MAKES 6 DOZEN

1¼ cups whole wheat flour

1 cup mesquite meal

½ cup cornmeal

¼ cup finely ground sunflower seeds

¼ cup vegetable oil

½ cup water

2 teaspoons salt

Preheat oven to 400 degrees and lightly grease a cookie sheet.

Combine all ingredients in a large bowl. Mixture will be crumbly.

Roll out dough very thin, working with only a small amount of dough at a time. Cut into 2-inch circles (a juice glass works well).

Bake on prepared cookie sheet in preheated oven. After about 4 minutes, the crackers will begin to brown on the bottom. Remove from the oven, turn each one over with a spatula and bake another 2 minutes. Watch them closely. If they become overbrowned, they taste bitter.

Mesquite Broth

This sweet, caramel-like broth is the basis for many delicious recipes, some of which are given here; many others you will discover on your own. **MAKES 3 CUPS**

4 cups broken mesquite pods

2 quarts water

Take about 4 cups of broken mesquite pods and cover with 2 quarts of water. Bring to a boil, turn down the heat, and simmer for about an hour. Cool.

Next, put your hands into the broth and wring and tear the pods in the broth, stirring and mashing the sweet pith into the liquid. The object is to get as much of the pith into the broth as possible.

Strain the liquid through a fine wire-mesh strainer and discard the seeds and fiber. Simmer the liquid uncovered until reduced to 3 cups.

Mesquite Pumpkin Pudding

Mesquite meal and broth combined with pumpkin makes a lightly sweet dessert. If you'd prefer to have it sweeter, taste before you add the eggs. You can add more agave syrup or honey, tasting until you are satisfied. This pudding can also serve as a pie filling if baked in a graham cracker or traditional pie crust.

Hint: Instead of throwing away your Halloween pumpkin, bake or steam it, scoop out the flesh, and use it right away or freeze for holiday meals. Typical jack-o'-lantern pumpkins are watery, so drain the cooked flesh in a strainer. **MAKES 6 TO 8 SERVINGS**

1¾ cups mashed pumpkin, fresh or canned

¼ cup fine mesquite meal

¼ cup Mesquite Broth (page 94)

1 can (12 ounces) evaporated milk

1 teaspoon ground cinnamon

2 to 4 tablespoons agave syrup or honey

2 beaten eggs

Preheat oven to 350 degrees.

Combine pumpkin, mesquite meal, mesquite broth, evaporated milk, cinnamon, and 2 tablespoons of agave syrup or honey in food processor bowl or in a deep bowl for use with an electric mixer. Taste and add additional sweetener if you wish. Beat in eggs.

Pour into shallow casserole or pie dish and bake in preheated oven for 50 to 60 minutes or until the center appears firm and a knife inserted halfway between the rim and the center comes out clean.

Mesquite Mousse

You'll find that this dessert is so rich that most folks will want only a small serving, but always be prepared for a few requests for seconds.   MAKES 6 TO 8 SERVINGS

2 cups Mesquite Broth (page 94)

1 can (12 ounces) evaporated milk
    or 1½ cups half-and-half

½ cup water

6 tablespoons cornstarch

2 beaten eggs

¼ cup Praline pecan liqueur

Combine mesquite broth and milk or half-and-half in the top of a double boiler.

In a small bowl or cup, combine water and cornstarch and stir until smooth. Add to mesquite mixture. Cook over boiling water for 4 minutes. Remove from heat, cover, and let sit for 10 minutes.

Beat eggs in a bowl. Carefully add 1 cup of the mesquite mixture to the eggs, stirring constantly. Add this mixture to the remaining mesquite mixture and cook and stir over boiling water for 4 minutes. Slowly stir in the Praline liqueur.

Rinse a 1-quart mold with cold water. Pour mousse into mold and chill until set, about 4 hours. Unmold to serve. Or just chill in a bowl and scoop out to serve.

Gila Monster

The Gila Monster makes a perfect beverage for a Sunday brunch, or serve it as a substitute for dessert and after-dinner coffee. It looks especially inviting in clear glass mugs or tulip-shaped stem glasses. MAKES 6 SERVINGS

1½ cups cold coffee

2½ cups cold Mesquite Broth
    (page 94)

½ cup cold milk (cow, nut, or soy)

½ cup coffee liqueur (optional)

Whipped cream

Cinnamon powder

Combine all liquids in a pitcher or large bowl. Pour into glasses or cups. Top with whipped cream and a dusting of cinnamon powder.

SUGGESTION: This recipe can be varied to individual tastes. Adjust the proportions of the liquid ingredients, or substitute other liqueurs such as crème de cacao, Praline pecan liqueur, or brandy.

Mesquite Jelly

This is the classic recipe used for years. **MAKES SIX TO SEVEN 6-OUNCE JARS**

2½ quarts mature, dried mesquite
  pods
Water
1 box (1.75 ounces) powdered fruit
  pectin (such as Sure-Jell)
4½ cups sugar
4 teaspoons lemon juice
Red food coloring (optional)

Break each mesquite pod into several pieces, place in a large kettle, and add water to cover. Simmer until liquid turns yellow. Work the mass several times with a potato masher. Pour juice through a fine wire-mesh strainer into a bowl. You will need 3 cups of juice.

While pods are boiling, sterilize jars and lids by boiling them for 15 minutes. Remove from water and drain.

Place prepared juice in a kettle or large saucepan and stir in powdered fruit pectin. Cook and stir over high heat until mixture comes to a full boil. Add sugar and lemon juice and return to a boil. Stirring constantly, boil for 1 minute or until syrup comes off metal spoon in a sheet. Remove from heat.

Skim off foam with metal spoon. If desired, a drop of red food coloring may be added. Pour quickly into sterilized jars or glasses. Cover at once with hot lids and screw rims on tightly.

Mesquite Bean Syrup and Recipes

Mesquite bean syrup is another way to add the mesquite flavor to foods. Several entrepreneurs have done the work for you and their products can be found online. In Tucson, Cheri's Desert Harvest has added mesquite syrup to its line of desert products; in southern New Mexico, Al and Jane Smoake are manufacturing mesquite syrup through A & J Family Farms; and in Texas, Take Thyme Teas is transforming some of that state's abundant mesquite crop into syrup. But here's a recipe if you'd like to give it a try yourself.

Mesquite Bean Syrup

This recipe comes from Jane and Al Smoake, who run A & J Family Farms just outside Socorro, New Mexico. They make prickly pear and mesquite products for sale at farmers' markets, craft shows, and gift shops throughout New Mexico and by mail order.

In a show of support for hometown entrepreneurs, the Socorro Heritage and Visitor Center coordinated some grants to help the Smoakes renovate a workshop into a certified kitchen in which to make their products.

Cooking the mesquite syrup is a two-step process—first making the extract, then combining that with sugar and a thickener to make the syrup.   **MAKES ABOUT 7 PINTS**

Mesquite Bean Extract

MAKES ABOUT 6 CUPS

3 pounds mature, dried mesquite beans

9 cups filtered water

Snap and rinse the mesquite beans, then place in a large stockpot with the water. Bring to a boil. Cover and simmer for 1½ hours.

Filter through a ricer or fine wire-mesh strainer and then a paper filter. Refrigerate if not to be used right away.

Mesquite Bean Syrup

MAKES ABOUT 7 PINTS

6 cups Mesquite Bean Extract
 (page 97)
3 tablespoons powdered fruit
 pectin (such as Sure-Jell)
9 cups granulated sugar

Sterilize 7 pint jars and lids by boiling in water for 15 minutes.

Add the Mesquite Bean Extract to a large stockpot. Begin heating over high heat. When the extract is hot, add the powdered fruit pectin and stir until dissolved.

Bring to a boil. Add the sugar. Cook for about 20 minutes. Pour into sterilized jars and seal.

Mesquite Salad Dressing

Many salad dressing recipes use honey. The mesquite syrup gives the same sweetness but also another layer of flavor. MAKES 1¼ CUPS

¼ cup Mesquite Bean Syrup
 (above or purchased)
½ cup olive oil
½ cup vinegar
¼ teaspoon Italian seasoning

Combine all ingredients in a jar and shake vigorously.

Mesquite-Glazed Sweet Potatoes

Cheri Romanoski, who is behind all the wonderful products from Cheri's Desert Harvest, developed this recipe to use her mesquite bean syrup.　MAKES 6 TO 8 SERVINGS

6 medium sweet potatoes or yams

½ cup Mesquite Bean Syrup (page 98 or purchased)

½ cup apple cider

1 tablespoon unsalted butter

¼ teaspoon cinnamon

¼ cup slivered almonds

Preheat oven to 350 degrees.

Put potatoes in a large saucepan and cover with water. Cook potatoes until nearly tender; peel and slice into a baking dish 10 by 6 by 1½ inches.

In a small saucepan combine the syrup, cider, butter, and cinnamon and heat until butter has melted and mixture is just warm (do not boil). Pour over potatoes and sprinkle with almonds.

Bake in preheated oven for 45 minutes, basting occasionally.

Cheri's Mesquite Brisket

In this recipe, you use the mesquite syrup as a marinade. The recipe was developed by Cheri Romanoski of Cheri's Desert Harvest.　MAKES 4 TO 6 SERVINGS

2 pounds beef brisket

Freshly ground black pepper

Garlic powder

1 cup Mesquite Bean Syrup (page 98 or purchased)

1 cup water

¼ cup olive oil

Trim excess fat from brisket; season meat with black pepper and garlic powder.

Mix syrup, water, and olive oil in a large resealable bag and add meat. Marinate for 2 to 4 hours in the refrigerator. Drain and pat dry with paper towels.

Grill over hot coals until desired doneness.

. . . .

Algarrobina, prominent in the next two recipes, is a dark molasses-like product manufactured in Peru from concentrated mesquite.

Algarrobina Cocktail

A celebration in Peru isn't complete without algarrobina cocktails. There are as many recipes for this Peruvian drink as there are bartenders in Peru; this is one option.

   The cocktail traditionally calls for a raw egg yolk. Either eliminate the egg yolk or use it if you trust the source and freshness of your eggs. Also wash the exterior of the eggshell before cracking.

MAKES 2 SERVINGS

6 ounces Pisco (see note)

2 ounces algarrobina syrup

2 ounces evaporated milk or
   half-and-half

2 teaspoons sugar

1 egg yolk

6 ice cubes

Cinnamon powder

Mix all ingredients in a blender for 1 minute at maximum speed.
   Divide into two glasses and decorate with cinnamon powder.

NOTE: Pisco is a brandy or aguardiente distilled from the white muscat grapes grown in Peru or Chile.

Algarrobina Pecan Pie

This recipe was developed by R. Roy Johnson, a Tucson biologist, when we were part of a nonprofit group attempting to promote mesquite in all forms.

Choose either white or dark Karo syrup depending on how strong you like the flavor to be. If you don't like maple flavor, substitute another liquid sweetener such as honey or even agave syrup.

MAKES ONE DEEP 9-INCH OR REGULAR 10-INCH PIE

4 eggs

½ cup plus 2 tablespoons white sugar

½ cup plus 2 tablespoons firmly packed brown sugar

2 tablespoons mesquite meal

1 tablespoon whole wheat flour

¾ cup Karo syrup

¼ cup algarrobina syrup

2 tablespoons maple syrup (or substitute another sweetener)

2 tablespoons honey

3 tablespoons unsalted butter, melted

1½ teaspoons vanilla extract

1 tablespoon cider vinegar

2 cups pecan halves

1 prepared unbaked deep 9-inch or regular 10-inch pie crust

Preheat oven to 375 degrees.

In a large mixing bowl, beat the eggs lightly.

In a small bowl combine sugars, mesquite meal, and flour, then add to eggs and combine.

Add syrups, honey, melted butter, vanilla extract, and vinegar. Stir to combine. Stir in pecans and pour into pie crust.

Cover top of pie loosely with sheet of aluminum foil, place on cookie sheet, and put on middle rack of preheated 375-degree oven for 15 minutes. Remove foil and reduce heat to 350 degrees for 45 more minutes. Check every 15 minutes and replace foil if pecans or crust start to burn. Turn off oven after 1 hour and leave pie in oven while it cools.

Piñon Nuts

The piñon pine does not offer its treasure easily—each rich, buttery nugget is nestled inside a pine cone. Although culinarily classified as a nut, biologists consider what we call a piñon nut actually a seed since it has no fruit associated with it. But for our purposes, we're going to call them nuts.

Piñon pines (*Pinus edulis*) grow throughout Arizona, New Mexico, Colorado, and Utah at elevations of from 4,000 to 8,000 feet. A closely associated species grows in California and Nevada as well as lower areas of Arizona. Its nut is a little larger with a softer shell and is sometimes called the Great Basin piñon nut. Purists maintain they can tell a decided difference in the flavor of the nuts from the two species.

The piñon pine is a foundation in mid-elevation Southwest ecosystems. A piñon forest can support a wildlife community, prevent erosion and floods, regulate runoff into rivers, and absorb carbon dioxide, one of the gases blamed for climate change. It takes a piñon nut two years to develop, and there is a good crop of piñon nuts only every three to seven years. With the widespread western drought in this century, bark beetles have killed wide swaths of piñon pines, depressing the harvest further.

Ecologists studying piñon pines at the University of Arizona's Biosphere 2 lab have determined that piñon pine trees will die faster and in greater numbers as rising temperatures from global warming intensify the effects of even short droughts. It is possible that an increase of only about 7 degrees could trigger piñon die-offs. Many climate studies say temperatures could rise that much by the end of the century.

If widespread die-offs occur over and over, the forests might never fully recover, resulting in the collapse of not only the piñons but also the ecosystems they support.

If you have some land or a yard that will support piñon pines, consider planting some to help support the species. They won't begin producing nuts in your lifetime, but you'll certainly help the planet. Penny

Frazier, who goes by the name Piñon Penny and is a tireless advocate for the trees, says, "Eating something makes the food a part of us, and us responsible for the species."

Piñon nuts are definitely a high-calorie food, with about 760 calories a cup. Mother Nature took care of us by slowing down our eating—cracking each nut's shell with your teeth and separating out the shells limits consumption considerably. The calories are spread over 39 percent carbohydrates, 5 percent protein, and 57 percent fat. They are a good source of vitamin E and manganese.

All Native American groups in the Southwest relished piñon nuts when they were available. With their high nutrition and pleasant flavor, finely ground piñon nuts mixed with a little water were used as a weaning food by early Havasupai mothers living at the bottom of the Grand Canyon.

Gathering Piñon Nuts

During summer hikes, you can scope out areas of trees that might have lots of cones then come back in September or October to do your picking. Gathering the nuts can be a messy business because of the pitch. Go prepared with gloves and something to cover your hair.

If it looks like the cones have opened, spread a tarp under the tree and hit the limbs gently to dislodge the unshelled nuts. If you are going to gather the unopened cones, bring a ladder and gently twist off the cones. Be careful with the branches—it is counterproductive to cut them off. Put the unopened cones in a gunnysack or lay them on a tarp in the sun until they dry and open. You can then shake out the nuts.

Storing Your Nuts

Keep your nuts in the shell, dry, and refrigerated. Once the nuts are out of the shell, they tend to go rancid—so eat them up. This should not be a problem!

Roasting and Shelling the Nuts

Once you've spent hours gathering your nuts, you want to make sure you don't ruin them or let them spoil before you have a chance to eat them. Since you may have picked them off the ground or gotten dirt on them in other ways, rinse them in a colander first while you preheat the oven to 325 degrees.

It is generally accepted that the roasting process is an art, not a science. Spread the unshelled nuts one layer deep on a cookie sheet or other baking pan. Since you won't know how much moisture is in the nut kernels, you'll have to test them for doneness as you go along. (Figure that nuts gathered earlier in the season will have more moisture.)

Roast for about 10 minutes, then crack a nut to test one kernel to see how it is coming. During the roasting the color of the kernel will change from white to translucent then back to white and then a pale manila color. The pale manila color is what you are aiming for.

At this point, or just before, remove them from the oven. Better to have them a little under-roasted than to waste all your energy by burning them.

Penny Frazier suggests spreading a dish towel on a flat surface, putting the hot nuts on top, and topping with another towel. Roll with a rolling pin to crack the shells. You'll have to experiment to get the right pressure. Store shelled nuts in the refrigerator as they can turn rancid quickly.

Piñon-Nut Butter

This simple but delicious recipe comes from the Santa Fe School of Cooking, right in the heart of piñon territory. Great on grainy whole wheat toast. **MAKES ABOUT ¾ CUP**

½ cup salted butter, softened

1 tablespoon honey

½ cup toasted piñon nuts

With a wooden spoon, cream butter and honey together in a small bowl.

Pulse piñon nuts in a food processor until fine, but not a paste. Stir into the butter mixture.

Put it into a pretty crock and use immediately. Or if you want a more elegant presentation, lay out a piece of plastic wrap. Form the butter into a log and roll in the plastic wrap. Refrigerate or freeze until you want to serve it, then slice into rounds. Piñon butter can be frozen for several weeks.

Piñon-Nut Pancakes

MAKES TWELVE 4-INCH PANCAKES

½ cup shelled piñon nuts

1 cup whole wheat or unbleached
all-purpose flour

1 teaspoon baking powder

½ teaspoon salt

2 tablespoons sugar

1 beaten egg

1¼ cups milk (cow, nut, or soy)

Chop the piñon nuts with a knife or nut chopper until fine. Set aside.

Combine the flour, baking powder, salt, and sugar in a blender jar or bowl. Add the beaten egg and milk and blend or stir to mix. Add the reserved nuts and blend or stir in.

Heat a lightly greased griddle or frying pan over medium heat until a drop of water bounces before evaporating.

Using a ¼-cup measure, ladle pancake batter onto the hot griddle or frying pan. When bubbles cover the tops of the pancakes, turn them over and cook until undersides are lightly browned.

Serve with maple syrup, honey, agave syrup, or jam.

Piñon-Nut Dressing

This recipe comes from Piñon Penny. While you can use it to flavor a hearty salad, I prefer it on vegetables.

MAKES ABOUT 1 CUP

¼ cup piñon nuts

¼ cup rice vinegar

¼ cup soy sauce

¼ cup water

1 tablespoon sugar

2 teaspoons dry mustard

Grind piñon nuts in a blender. Add the vinegar, soy sauce, water, sugar, and mustard; blend well.

Piñon Corn Muffins

This unusual muffin recipe comes from Phyllis Hogan of the Winter Sun Trading Company, located in Flagstaff, Arizona. Winter Sun specializes in traditional organic Southwest herbs. Hogan co-founded the Arizona Ethnobotanical Research Association to preserve knowledge of traditional plant use in Arizona and the greater Southwest.

The *quotsvii* (Hopi cooking ash) is made on Third Mesa on the Hopi Reservation by burning dried branches of four-wing saltbush (*Atriplex canescens*) or various species of juniper in an outside fire pit with a screen underneath to collect the ash. The ash provides important minerals. If you'd like to use it instead of the baking powder, you can obtain quotsvii from Winter Sun; note that you may have to call to inquire because they may have too little available to list on their website.   **MAKES 12 MUFFINS**

1 cup white corn flour, coarsely ground

1 cup whole wheat flour

2 pinches cinnamon

1 pinch nutmeg

1 teaspoon baking powder or 1 teaspoon quotsvii (Hopi cooking ash)

½ cup piñon nuts, shelled

1 large organic, free-range chicken egg

½ cup melted coconut oil, plus a little more to oil muffin cups

½ cup finely diced organic apple or ½ cup fresh organic applesauce

Preheat oven to 400 degrees. Grease muffin cups with coconut oil.

In a medium bowl, first mix together all of the dry ingredients, including piñon nuts.

In a separate bowl, whip together the egg and ½ cup melted coconut oil. Add to dry ingredients. Stir in diced apple or applesauce. Stir until ingredients are combined, but do not beat or overmix. Divide the batter among the 12 muffin cups.

At high elevation, bake in preheated oven 17 to 20 minutes; at low elevation, bake 15 minutes.

Pumpkin-Piñon Bread

When the weather turns cool, this is perfect for breakfast or snacks. Use fresh pumpkin (perhaps the jack-o'-lantern?—see page 94) or canned. With the high vitamin A content, it is also good for lunchboxes. If the kids have helped cut and steam the pumpkin or hunted the nuts, they'll be interested, even if this is an unfamiliar flavor. **MAKES 2 LOAVES**

1 cup shelled piñon nuts

3 cups unbleached all-purpose
   flour

2 teaspoons baking powder

½ teaspoon nutmeg

1 teaspoon cinnamon

½ teaspoon salt

1¾ cups cooked pumpkin

1½ cups firmly packed light
   brown sugar

3 eggs, lightly beaten

½ cup unsalted butter, melted

Preheat oven to 350 degrees. Grease two 5- by 9-inch loaf pans and set aside.

Put the piñon nuts on an ungreased cookie sheet in the preheated oven for about 10 minutes while you prepare the rest of the recipe.

Sift flour, baking powder, nutmeg, cinnamon, and salt together into a medium bowl.

In a separate bowl, mix together remaining ingredients and add to flour mixture. Stir just until blended; don't overbeat. Remove piñons from oven and stir into the batter.

Pour batter into the two greased loaf pans and bake at 350 degrees for about 1 hour or until a toothpick inserted in the center comes out clean. Cool loaf pans on rack.

Russian Pine-Nut Vodka

This amusing recipe is taken with permission from Piñon Penny's website, Goods from the Woods. I haven't tried it yet. The essential oils in the shells flavor the vodka. In Russia, vodka flavored with the nuts from the Siberian pine is called *kedrovka*.   **FLAVORS 1 BOTTLE OF VODKA**

1 bottle vodka, ⅔ full
Pine nuts in the shell

Pour out one-third of the vodka and save for another use. Fill the remaining space in the bottle with pine nuts. They will fall to the bottom. Close the cap and put it on a dark shelf for at least 3 weeks. When you see it next, it will be dark as brandy or darker. The longer you keep the nuts in the bottle, the darker it will get.

There is no need to filter or do anything with it but to drink in small shots. But make sure before you drink, you chill it in the refrigerator; some people place it in the freezer for an hour, where it will become very thick, with a concentrated pine-nut smell and taste.

Some people eat the nuts after the vodka is consumed—one can get drunk just from doing that. There is a belief that consuming a half ounce of kedrovka before every dinner will keep you healthy forever (and certainly happy for a while).

Quinoa Pilaf with Piñon Nuts and Cranberries

This is nice enough for company, but easy enough for everyday fare. Toasting the piñon nuts enhances their flavor.   MAKES 4 TO 6 SERVINGS

6 tablespoons piñon nuts

1 cup quinoa

1 tablespoon olive oil

½ cup finely chopped onion

1 tablespoon finely grated
   orange zest

2 cups water

½ cup dried cranberries

½ cup finely chopped parsley

Salt and freshly ground black
   pepper

Toast piñon nuts in a dry frying pan until lightly browned. Set aside.

Put the quinoa in a fine strainer and rinse under running water for several seconds, tossing so all grains are rinsed. Drain.

Heat oil in a medium-size heavy saucepan over moderately low heat. Add onion and cook, stirring until softened. Stir in drained quinoa and zest and combine. Add water and bring to a boil. Reduce heat to low and cook, covered, until liquid is absorbed, about 20 minutes. (You will see a tiny white ring on each grain of quinoa.)

Stir in dried cranberries, parsley, and piñon nuts. Add salt and pepper to taste.

Tomatoes with Greens and Piñon Nuts

MAKES 4 LARGE OR 8 SMALL SERVINGS

4 large Roma tomatoes, halved
   lengthwise and seeded

Salt

2 tablespoons olive oil

3 garlic cloves, minced

2 to 3 cups chopped wild greens
   or spinach

½ teaspoon dried thyme or
   oregano

Freshly ground black pepper

1½ teaspoons unsalted butter

3 tablespoons piñon nuts

Sprinkle cut sides of tomatoes with salt. Drain the tomatoes cut sides down on a rack set over paper towels for 30 minutes.

Heat the olive oil in a 12-inch heavy skillet over moderately high heat until hot but not smoking. Add tomato halves, cut sides down, and cook for 3 or 4 minutes. Turn tomato halves. Cover pan and cook until just softened but not browned, another 4 to 5 minutes. Transfer tomatoes, cut side up, to a platter. When cool enough to touch, use a teaspoon and paring knife to cut out the soft, seedy interiors; set these aside in a bowl.

Add garlic to pan and sauté over low heat until just browned. Add greens and tomato insides and stir until greens are wilted and tomato liquid has evaporated. Season with the thyme or oregano and salt and pepper. Divide the greens mixture among the tomato halves.

Wipe the frying pan with a paper towel. Add the butter and melt over medium heat. Add piñon nuts and cook, stirring, until golden, 1 to 2 minutes. Sprinkle the nuts on top of the greens.

Chia

Chia, a member of the mint family, is one of the oldest human foods in the Americas, dating back as early as 3500 BCE. Yet it was virtually forgotten until the last few decades. Most Americans knew chia only as the little seeds that grow green "fur" for Chia Pets.

When the Spanish made contact with the Aztecs, chia was one of the most important crops. But like amaranth, it was used in rituals the Spanish Catholics wished to suppress, so the cultivation was largely curtailed. It survived in isolated pockets, however, and in more remote areas of northern Mexico among the Tarahumara, Yaqui, and Mayo groups.

Farther north in what is now the American Southwest, many of the Indian groups gathered chia from plants growing in the wild. Among the groups documented as using chia in Arizona were several groups of Apaches; the Pima, Mohave, Hualapai, Chemehuevi, Quechan, and Paiute; as well as the Hia-Ced O'odham. In California, it was popular among the Coahuila (Cahuilla).

The species of chia grown to the south and most of what is available commercially is *Salvia hispanica*. The seeds grow on longish flower spikes. In the American Southwest, the species is *Salvia columbariae* and the flowers are more ball shaped and there may be several—one atop the other on a single stem.

Chia grows in granite soils, disturbed gravel, and sandy washes. It appears with other spring flowers, like California poppies, from March to early May.

So why the great interest in these little black seeds? Christina Pirello noted on the Huffington Post's website that chia seeds "could well be nature's perfect food." And they certainly have many healthful properties. To begin with, they are high in fiber and when mixed with water they exhibit the mucilaginous polysaccharides that are so helpful in controlling blood sugar.

Chia is also high in omega-3 fatty acids, 60 percent of which is alpha-linolenic acid. Human beings evolved on a diet high in both omega-3 and omega-6 fatty acids. But today our modern diets are out of balance, with a much higher portion of omega-6 fatty acids—in large part from eating grains and meat and dairy products from animals fed on grain rather than grass.

Chia seeds are a source of protein, are high in antioxidants, and are rich in boron, which aids in the absorption of calcium, needed for strong teeth and bones. Unlike flaxseed, which is also promoted as a good source of omega-3 acids, chia does not need to be refrigerated and the benefits are available from both whole and ground seeds. With not much flavor of their own, they are easily incorporated in many dishes to boost the nutrition level.

Chia Breakfast Parfait

The inspiration for this recipe comes from my friend Susan Adler, who frequently has this for breakfast. It supplies a healthy serving of protein to start your day, plus fruit for antioxidants and a satisfying crunch without a carb overload.

   Mix the fresh fruit—blueberries and diced peaches or blackberries and diced strawberries. Mixed frozen berries work well in the winter when fresh fruits are scarce. I find that this breakfast keeps me feeling full until lunch. **MAKES 1 SERVING**

¾ cup low-fat plain or vanilla
   yogurt
3 tablespoons granola
½ cup berries or diced fruit
3 teaspoons chia seed

In the bottom of a parfait glass, layer ¼ cup yogurt, then sprinkle in 1 tablespoon of granola, ⅓ of the fruit, and 1 teaspoon of chia seed. Repeat twice, using all the ingredients.

Chia Fruit Smoothie

MAKES 2 SERVINGS

1 tablespoon chia seed
½ cup plus 1 tablespoon cold
   water
½ cup plain or vanilla low-fat or
   nonfat yogurt
1 soft, ripe banana
½ cup berries of your choice
½ cup cold milk (cow, nut, or soy)
½ cup cold fruit juice
4 or 5 ice cubes

In a small bowl, combine chia seed and water and let sit for about 15 minutes to form a gel. In a blender jar, combine chia gel and all other ingredients. Blend until well combined.

Chia Fruit Salad

Martha Burgess, "Muffin" to her many friends, is a teacher, wild-food advocate, and purveyor of southwestern foods and cultural items. She was an early advocate of chia and developed this recipe. It was printed in the Native Seeds/SEARCH recipe book *From Furrow to Fire*. She suggests trying apples, blueberries, and bananas along with fresh-squeezed orange juice.

She has worked with Native American youngsters, helping to educate them in the healthy ways of their ancestors. When this salad sits for a while, the chia seeds cause it to gel. Muffin told the children that it was "Tohono O'odham Jell-O." MAKES 6 TO 8 SERVINGS

2 tablespoons chia seeds

¼ cup fruit juice of your choice

4 or 5 cups of fruit of your choice

Add chia seeds and fruit juice to your favorite fruit salad combination. Let sit 45 minutes for chia seeds to gel. Serve chilled.

Chia Applesauce-Banana Muffins

These healthy muffins include whole grain, two fruits, and all the benefits of the chia seeds. Grind the seeds in a coffee grinder or blender.

The muffins are very lightly sweet and are good for breakfast with jam or they can round out a hearty soup along with some cheese for a satisfying light supper. I served them with goat cheese to accompany thick mushroom soup. MAKES 12 MUFFINS

1 cup whole wheat flour

1 cup unbleached all-purpose flour

¼ cup firmly packed brown sugar

2 teaspoons baking powder

1 teaspoon baking soda

¼ teaspoon cinnamon

¼ teaspoon salt

6 tablespoons ground chia seeds

¾ cup mashed bananas

½ cup unsweetened applesauce

1 beaten egg

2 tablespoons molasses

2 tablespoons canola oil

1 tablespoon milk (cow, nut, or soy)

Preheat oven to 350 degrees. Grease 12 muffin cups or line with paper cups.

In a large bowl whisk together all the dry ingredients, including chia seeds.

In a medium bowl, combine remaining ingredients. Add the wet ingredients to the dry ingredients, stirring just until combined. Don't beat.

Fill the muffin cups and bake in the preheated oven for 17 to 20 minutes.

Chia Energy Bars

Stick these in your backpack for a great snack during a long hike or bike ride. For storage you can wrap the individual bars in plastic wrap or aluminum foil and freeze.   **MAKES 24 BARS**

2 cups uncooked oatmeal

½ cup chia seeds

½ cup chopped almonds

¼ cup unsalted sunflower seeds

½ cup raisins

¼ cup dried cranberries

¼ cup chopped dried apricots

¾ cup unbleached all-purpose
flour

½ cup firmly packed brown sugar

1 teaspoon cinnamon

1 teaspoon baking soda

¼ teaspoon salt

½ cup vegetable oil

1 large egg

1 cup unsweetened applesauce

1 teaspoon vanilla extract

Preheat oven to 350 degrees. Grease a 9- by 13-inch baking pan.

In a large bowl, combine oatmeal, chia seeds, almonds, sunflower seeds, dried fruits, flour, sugar, cinnamon, baking soda, and salt.

In another bowl, whisk together oil, egg, applesauce, and vanilla extract. Add wet ingredients to the dry ingredients, stirring until evenly moistened.

Spread in prepared baking pan and bake for 35 to 40 minutes. Cool and cut into 24 bars.

Chia-Corn Waffles

The inspiration for this recipe came from many websites that suggest that athletes can benefit from a food that fuels the legendary runners of the Tarahumara tribe. The Tarahumara, who live in the mountains of northern Mexico, make a mixture of corn and chia that they eat by the pinch or mix in water to make a drink.

When my husband, Ford, tasted the first waffle off the waffle iron he said, "Wow! These don't need any syrup to make them delicious." Actually, he did dribble some maple syrup on his third one "just to see how it is." Use a soy or nut milk to make them vegan.   **MAKES FIVE 4-INCH WAFFLES**

¼ cup chia seeds

¾ cup water

¾ cup finely ground cornmeal
  or masa

¼ cup oat bran

½ teaspoon salt

1 teaspoon baking powder

½ cup milk (cow, nut, or soy)

1 tablespoon oil

2 tablespoons agave or maple
  syrup

1 teaspoon vanilla or almond
  extract

Cooking spray

Put the chia seeds in a 1-cup glass measuring cup and fill to the 1-cup mark with water. Let the chia seeds soak until they form a gel.

Meanwhile, in a large bowl, mix the cornmeal or masa, oat bran, salt, and baking powder. Stir to combine.

In another bowl combine the milk, oil, syrup, and extract and add to the dry ingredients. Add the gelled chia seeds and stir just to combine.

Heat waffle iron and spray with cooking spray. Bake the waffles about 4 to 5 minutes until nicely browned.

Aztec Delight

The recipe for Aztec Delight is the result of a Sunday-morning project I began to amuse myself. In their book *Chia: Rediscovering a Forgotten Crop of the Aztecs*, Ricardo Ayerza and Wayne Coates write that at the time of the arrival of Columbus in the New World, chia was one of the four main Aztec crops. One of the ways they used it was to make what the authors called a "dough," called *tzoalli*. They parched amaranth and chia seeds, ground them, and mixed them with black maguey syrup. So far everything sounded tasty, but chocolate was an Aztec favorite as well so I decided to include some of that. I began with just a small amount—you can always increase the recipe if you want to make a big batch.

Betcha can't eat just one! **MAKES ABOUT 20 TO 24 BALLS**

¼ cup chia seed

¼ cup amaranth seed

2 to 3 tablespoons agave syrup

½ cup semisweet chocolate chips

In a wok or heavy-bottomed pan over medium heat parch the chia seed for just a minute or two, stirring constantly. Transfer to a coffee grinder or blender and grind to a powder. Put into a bowl.

Repeat the parching and grinding process with the amaranth grain. It is possible the amaranth grain will pop in the pan, resulting in a light cloud, like very tiny popcorn kernels. If that happens, fine; if not, equally fine.

Combine the ground chia and amaranth in a bowl; add the agave syrup slowly, stirring until you have a stiff dough that holds together. Form into balls the size of a large olive.

Put the chocolate chips in a heatproof bowl and melt in the microwave or place in a double boiler and melt over hot water. If using the microwave, heat for 1 minute, check, then continue heating in 30-second increments until melted.

Line a plate with waxed paper or plastic wrap. Using the tines of a fork, roll each ball of the chia/amaranth dough in the chocolate. Transfer to the plate. Refrigerate until the chocolate has hardened.

Tepary Beans

Wild and domesticated tepary beans (*Phaseolus acutifolius*) have been around the Western Hemisphere for 5,000 years. While tepary beans today are grown agriculturally and this book deals with wild foods, the modern tepary is a domesticated wild crop and is so iconic to this area it really cannot be left out.

Many southwestern Indian tribes grew the beans, but none relied on them or relished them more than the Tohono O'odham of Arizona. *Tohono O'odham* means "Desert People," but it is not hard to understand why the O'odham were called by others "the Bean Eaters" when we realize that as late as 1940, the average O'odham consumed about three-quarters of a pound of beans daily. Teparies even figure in their creation myth. When the Tohono O'odham get together to recount their ancient stories, the children learn how the Milky Way was formed of white tepary beans many untold centuries ago.

Anglo-American farmers had a brief flirtation with tepary farming beginning around 1914 when the bean was introduced commercially into California. Other farmers in Arizona and New Mexico began cultivating the little bean when they heard that teparies are a nutritious crop adapted over centuries to dry-land farming. In wet years, teparies achieved or surpassed the average bean yield without irrigation, and in drought years teparies still produced a small crop when other crops failed completely.

These experimentations with tepary farming were before mass marketing and new-product-introduction techniques had been developed to their present levels, however, and though the beans grew in the field, they died in the marketplace. Farmers, who could not sell them, did not want to grow them. Then, before they really had a chance to catch on, gasoline-powered engines made it possible for farmers to suck up groundwater to irrigate their dry fields. Drought hardiness became an irrelevant issue, and when the farmers grew beans, they planted new hybrids instead.

Small-scale Mexican and Native American farmers began to turn to the hybrids as well, but also kept small plots of tepary beans. The older farmers, particularly, were reluctant to give up something that had been so important to their people.

The Native Americans' preference for tepary beans was based on more than emotional factors. I once talked to an elderly Tohono O'odham woman who said that in the past, tepary beans had been a particularly good traveling food because human beings could be well nourished by eating these beans just once a day, whereas they would require two servings of another kind of bean.

Since then, scientific analyses have shown us that teparies rank slightly higher than most other beans in protein and niacin and quite a lot higher in calcium, which is important for people who do not use dairy products (see tables 2 and 3). Teparies also have a low glycemic index, which protects people eating them from a dangerously rapid rise in blood glucose levels after meals. This is particularly important for the Native American populations where there is an extremely high rate of adult-onset diabetes (type 2 diabetes). Those who suffer from diabetes can reduce their need for insulin shots by eating plenty of teparies and other desert foods, such as prickly pear pads (nopales) and chia, that have the gums and fibers useful in controlling blood sugar.

With today's dwindling water resources, teparies are again attracting attention from commercial growers. Two Native American groups near Tucson are growing them—the San Xavier Cooperative Farm and the Tohono O'odham Community Action (TOCA) farm; there is a producer in Sacaton, south of Phoenix (the Button family at Ramona Farms), as well as one in Stockton, California (Rancho Gordo); and many farmers in northern Mexico have renewed interest in the bean. Unfortunately, many of the genetic strains and color variations have been lost over the years, although seed is still available for yellow, brown, beige, red-brown, white, black, and mottled varieties.

Mike Sheedy, a researcher with the University of Arizona's Maricopa Agricultural Center, has been experimenting with teparies since 2003. He has developed a black variety by culling black beans that occur spontaneously in the white crop and selectively planting those. He's also working on dark brown, pink, and speckled varieties.

Besides being drought tolerant, teparies set seed and mature quickly, taking full advantage of short wet periods, such as the summer monsoonal rains in Arizona. They are also tolerant of common bean blight. Some experiments have already done work in crossing teparies with other beans to promote these desirable traits.

TABLE 2. PROTEIN SCORES OF SEVERAL TEPARY-CEREAL COMBINATIONS

Whole Meal Combinations	Percentage Protein of the Diet	Protein Score*
Tepary 67%–Wheat 33%	21.1%	95
Tepary 67%–Corn 33%	17.4%	92
Tepary 50%–Wheat 50%	19.5%	93
Tepary 50%–Corn 50%	16.9%	97
Tepary 100%	25.0%	74
Wheat 100%	14.0%	56
Corn 100%	8.8%	46

* A score of 100 relates to a perfect-percentage amino acid pattern of a hypothetical protein assumed to be optimal for human growth and development by the Food and Agriculture Organization of the United Nations, Committee on Protein Requirements.
From J. C. Scheerens, A. M. Tinsley, I. R. Abbas, C. W. Weber, and J. W. Berry, "The Nutritional Significance of Tepary Bean Consumption," *Desert Plants* 5, no. 1 (1983):52.

TABLE 3. NUTRITIVE VALUE OF VARIOUS LEGUMES

Variety	Crude Protein	Crude Fat	Carbohydrates	Calories per 100 Grams
Tepary, wild	24.5%	1.4%	*	*
Tepary, domesticated	23.2%	0.8%	59.0%	320
Lima beans	19.7%	1.1%	64.8%	341
Kidney beans	22.1%	1.7%	61.4%	341
Lentils	24.2%	1.8%	60.8%	346
Garbanzos (chickpeas)	20.1%	4.5%	61.5%	358

* Not available.
Compiled from J. C. Scheerens, A. M. Tinsley, I. R. Abbas, C. W. Weber, and J. W. Berry, "The Nutritional Significance of Tepary Bean Consumption," *Desert Plants* 5, no. 1 (1983):11–14; tepary values are based on research by Gary Paul Nabhan.

Despite the fact that teparies cost double or triple what other beans go for, consumers seek out teparies. Native Seeds/SEARCH alone mails out hundreds of pounds a year, and Mike Sheedy produces 4,000 to 8,000 pounds a year and sells them out of the Phoenix area.

Properly cooked, teparies are as delicious as any other bean, and when combined in proportions of half and half with wheat or corn, the resulting protein score is just slightly less than that of eggs, the standard by which all proteins are measured. Teparies can be an important food for anyone trying to cut down on meat while maintaining a high-protein diet. The white ones taste similar to other small white beans, whereas the darker varieties have a heartier flavor.

Growing, Harvesting, and Cleaning

If you live in a dry climate and cannot find teparies for sale in your area, or if you find them a bit expensive, you might want to try growing your own. Native Seeds/SEARCH sells seeds for more than a dozen varieties and gives advice on growing them.

When most of the pods are dry on the plants in the fall, you can pull up the plants, roots and all, or cut off the tops of the plants and leave the roots, with their nitrogen-fixing nodules, in the ground to enrich the soil. Let the plants dry in the sun for about a week. When they are completely dry, you can spread them on a canvas and beat them with a stick to separate the pods from the plants and then the beans from the pods. On a breezy day, put the beans and small chaff on a tray and toss them into the wind over a canvas. The wind will blow away most of the chaff.

Cooking Hints

Because teparies seem to dry out more completely than other beans, it is essential that they be presoaked before cooking. Beans that have been stored awhile should soak about 12 hours. Doug Levy, chef-owner of Feast restaurant in Tucson, cuts down on cooking time dramatically by soaking the beans for two days in the refrigerator. Very fresh beans need less soaking and have even been known to start sprouting during a long soak. During the soaking, they will absorb quite a quantity of water. The more water they take up, the easier they will be to cook. You can figure that two cups of dried beans will swell to about five cups during soaking.

Although cooking times may vary widely depending on freshness of the beans, location of the field, type of tepary, and other yet-undiscovered factors, it can generally be assumed that teparies will take considerably longer to cook than other beans.

With a heavy cast-iron pot or an electric slow cooker, plan on eight to fourteen hours of cooking, although beans stored for many years may take even longer. A pressure cooker will complete the job in anywhere from a half hour to an hour and fifteen minutes. Never fill a pressure cooker more than half full and use at least two quarts of water.

Some bean cooking experts suggest bringing water to a boil in a pot and then adding the beans as a method of quickly softening the seed coat. If you find you must add water during cooking, it should be hot water because reduction in cooking temperature seems to have a toughening effect on the beans. Also, salt should be added only toward the end of the cooking time as it also toughens the beans.

You should also understand that a tepary bean that has finally become soft is not necessarily a fully cooked bean. You must continue cooking the teparies until they have lost their starchy, raw flavor, which, with conventional methods, may be as long as two additional hours.

It is at this point that the fun starts. The following recipes are some suggestions for especially delicious uses for teparies. A creative cook can come up with many more.

Remember, however, that as with other beans, teparies should be fully cooked before the addition of salt, molasses, brown sugar, tomatoes, tomato sauce, ketchup, or vinegar. When added during cooking, these ingredients tend to harden the beans.

Although teparies do take considerably longer to prepare than most of our modern convenience foods, the extra time need not lie in the way of greater popular acceptance for these gifts from the Desert People. Whatever cooking method you prefer, it makes sense to cook three or four times as many beans as you will need for one day and divide the remainder into portions to be frozen for future fast-food meals.

If the following two bean combinations find their way into the lunchbox, they can be called sandwich spreads. If they are used as hors d'oeuvres, they can take the dressed-up name of "pâté." For presentation as an appetizer, serve with small pickles (or gherkins) sliced lengthwise and crisp crackers or crusty French bread.

Tepary Vegetarian Pâté

When my friend Suzann Lark was a chef at the Canyon Ranch health resort in Tucson, she was invited to be a guest chef for a dinner at the James Beard House in New York City. She modified and improved my recipe for Tepary Pâté and prepared it as an appetizer for her dinner. This is nice served with crackers or thin slices of toasted French bread.   MAKES ABOUT 6 CUPS

1 cup chopped celery

1 cup chopped carrots

1 cup chopped onion

1 tablespoon minced garlic

1 tablespoon extra virgin olive oil

½ cup sunflower seeds

2 cups cooked tepary beans

2 tablespoons light soy sauce

2 tablespoons minced fresh basil
   (or 1 tablespoon dried)

¼ teaspoon dried oregano

¼ teaspoon cumin

2 tablespoons minced jalapeños

¼ teaspoon freshly ground black
   pepper

Sauté celery, carrots, onion, and garlic in olive oil until tender.

Grind sunflower seeds to a meal in a food processor.

Add cooked vegetables, beans, and flavorings to the processor bowl and process until smooth.

White Tepary and Pork Spread

MAKES ABOUT 4 CUPS

1 medium-size carrot

1 rib celery

1 small onion

1 pork chop (about 4 ounces)

1½ cups cooked white tepary
   beans

1 bay leaf

½ teaspoon dried thyme leaves

¼ cup dry white wine

Salt and freshly ground black
   pepper

Coarsely chop carrot, celery, and onion. Place in a heavy covered saucepan with the pork chop, beans, bay leaf, and thyme. Add water just to cover. Bring to a boil over medium heat, then reduce heat to a simmer and cover.

When pork and vegetables are done (about 20 minutes), remove pork, beans, and vegetables and reserve; discard bay leaf. Add wine to broth. Boil uncovered and stir often until liquid evaporates to about ¼ cup.

De-bone meat and chop coarsely. Whirl in a food processor or blender until fine. Add the beans, vegetables, and reduced broth from the saucepan and process until very smooth. Add salt and pepper to taste.

Tepary-Basil Appetizer

This is a simple summer appetizer to make when your basil plants are full and bushy.

For a party, I cut the baguette into diagonal slices, spread them with the tepary-basil mixture, then garnish half of the slices with a purchased mixed-olive tapenade and half with a purchased sundried-tomato relish and arrange them alternately on a large platter. The colorful combination makes a lovely presentation. **MAKES ABOUT 2 CUPS OF SPREAD**

1 cup cooked tepary beans

1 cup loosely packed basil leaves

1 tablespoon olive oil

Bean cooking liquid (or water)
   to moisten

1 baguette

GARNISHES

Purchased mixed-olive tapenade

Purchased sundried-tomato relish
   (or other red spread)

Combine cooked teparies, basil leaves, and olive oil in the bowl of a food processor. Add a little of the bean cooking liquid or water and process. If necessary, add more bean liquid or water, tablespoon by tablespoon, until of thick spreading consistency.

Slice baguette. Place slices on a cookie sheet and toast in a 350 degree oven just a few minutes on each side until lightly crisp.

Spread tepary paste on the toast slices. Top with mixed-olive tapenade or sundried-tomato relish.

Tepary Salad in Lettuce Cups

The presentation raises this simple salad to something special. **MAKES ABOUT 1¼ CUPS OF SALAD**

1 cup cooked tepary beans

¼ cup minced onion

½ cup finely shredded purple
   cabbage

½ cup shredded carrot

⅛ teaspoon chipotle powder

1 to 2 tablespoons Italian dressing

¼ teaspoon powdered garlic

Salt and freshly ground black
   pepper to taste

Iceberg lettuce

Combine all ingredients except lettuce in a bowl.

Core the lettuce and carefully separate the leaves. You want nice, intact bowls.

Divide the bean mixture among the lettuce leaves. As people eat, they will wrap each leaf around the beans, tucking in the edges if possible. Some leaves will be more pliable than others.

Tepary Bean and Tuna Salad

This is a variation on a classic. Great for a potluck. For home, you can just stir it up in a bowl and serve with lettuce, but to make it fancier, arrange a bed of baby spinach on a platter, pile up the salad in the center, and garnish with cherry tomatoes and olives. The recipe is easily doubled or tripled to serve more people.   MAKES 2 TO 4 SERVINGS

1 cup cooked white tepary beans

1 can (7 ounces) solid white albacore tuna in water, drained

½ cup sliced green onions with some green

2 tablespoons fresh lemon juice

3 tablespoons Dijon mustard

⅓ cup olive oil

Cherry tomatoes (optional garnish)

Pitted olives (optional garnish)

In a medium bowl combine the tepary beans, the drained tuna, and the green onions.

In a cup or small bowl, combine the lemon juice and mustard. With a small whisk or a fork, whisk in the olive oil. Stir the dressing into the tuna and bean mixture.

Three Sisters Soup

The "Three Sisters" are the mainstays of early Native American diets: corn, beans, and squash. This soup is easy and delicious. You can use any type of summer squash—yellow crookneck, zucchini, or Mexican gray. **MAKES 6 SERVINGS**

1 teaspoon olive oil

1 small onion, diced

1 clove garlic, minced

1 cup diced summer squash

1 cup cooked corn kernels

1 cup cooked tepary beans

4 cups chicken or vegetable broth

1 teaspoon crumbled Mexican
    oregano

1 to 2 chiltepins (optional)

Salt and freshly ground black
    pepper

In a large pot heat olive oil and sauté onion until translucent. Add garlic and sauté one minute. Add diced summer squash and sauté until just tender. Add corn kernels and beans and stir. Add broth, oregano, chiltepins if using, and salt and pepper to taste and heat through.

Layered Tepary Enchiladas

The combination of teparies, corn, and cheese makes this dish rich in protein without meat. **SERVES 2**

Oil for frying

6 corn tortillas

2 cups cooked tepary beans

1 cup cooked corn kernels

1 small can (8 ounces) tomato
    sauce

Chile powder or paste, to taste

¼ teaspoon cumin or to taste

½ cup shredded longhorn or jack
    cheese

½ cup chopped green or black
    olives

3 cups shredded lettuce

Heat ¼ inch oil in small frying pan and fry tortillas one by one, briefly, until limp but not crisp. Remove and pat each with paper towel to absorb excess oil.

In a medium saucepan, combine teparies, corn kernels, and tomato sauce; heat. Season to taste with chile and cumin.

For each individual serving, place a tortilla on a plate, add a layer of the bean and corn mixture, then repeat twice, ending with beans. Top with shredded cheese and chopped olives and surround each tortilla stack with shredded lettuce.

All Wrong Chili

The reason this chili is "all wrong"—well, mostly wrong anyway—is that true chili aficionados never use beans in their chili. If some maverick does use beans, the choice is usually brown pintos or red kidneys. Most chili recipes call for red peppers, although green ones may sometimes be included as well. The meat is generally beef, although pork, venison, and even javelina (wild peccary) are sometimes used. All Wrong Chili uses beans (white teparies), green chiles only, and turkey. But the joke is on all the purists. This chili tastes great!

MAKES 6 TO 8 SERVINGS

5 cups cooked white tepary beans
and 1 cup cooking broth or
water
½ cup chopped onion
1 or 2 cloves garlic, minced
2 tablespoons oil
1 cup strong turkey broth
1 to 2 cups chopped or ground
cooked turkey
1 small can (4 ounces) diced green
chiles
½ teaspoon cumin
Salt and freshly ground black
pepper

Put cooked beans and 1 cup of the cooking broth or water into a medium-size covered saucepan and smash some of the beans against the side of the pot with the back of a spoon. Stir mashed beans into the bean broth or water to thicken it.

In a skillet, brown the chopped onion and minced garlic in the oil. Add to the beans along with the turkey broth, cooked turkey, green chiles, cumin, and salt and pepper to taste. Simmer 15 minutes to thicken and blend flavors.

Tepary Cassoulet

This recipe comes courtesy of Doug Levy, who serves it at his Tucson restaurant Feast. Levy is a creative and eclectic chef who changes his menu frequently to the delight of his ardent customers. Levy serves this dish with grilled lamb chops and pumpkin-seed brittle, but suggests it would be great with pork loin or tenderloin, pork sausage, or duck as well.

Generally, tepary beans take at least eight hours of cooking and sometimes much more to become soft, but Levy has shortened the cooking time by soaking the beans for two full days rather than overnight. I'd suggest playing it on the safe side—don't start this dish in the afternoon hoping to serve it for dinner that night. Make it the day before and if it needs longer cooking time, you can give it whatever it needs. You'd hate to have to send out for pizza for your guests. **MAKES 8 TO 10 SERVINGS**

1 pound tepary beans

1 large yellow onion

2 small carrots

2 stalks celery

6 slices bacon, cut into ¼-inch
    strips

Olive oil

1 tablespoon minced garlic

1 cup dry white wine

3 quarts chicken stock

Salt and freshly ground black
    pepper

Pick through the beans, making sure there are no stones in them, rinse them, and soak them for 2 days in the refrigerator in enough water to cover them by 2 inches. When you are ready to cook, drain the beans and rinse them.

Cut the onion, carrots, and celery into a *brunoise*, a very fine dice.

Put a heavy saucepan big enough to hold all the ingredients over medium heat and sauté the bacon until it begins to crisp.

Add the diced onions, carrots, and celery and just enough olive oil to coat them and sauté them until they begin to soften, about 8 to 10 minutes. Add the minced garlic and sauté another minute.

Add the wine and scrape up all the bits that may have stuck to the pot while they cooked, add the beans and the chicken stock, and bring to a boil. Reduce to a simmer and stir occasionally until the beans are cooked through, about 1½ hours. Check to see if the beans are very soft; if not, continue to cook. Season to taste with salt and pepper.

Tepary Bean Cakes

I used black teparies for these delicious patties, although white or brown teparies will work fine. You could serve one as a first course arranged on a small plate surrounded by the garnishes. Two or three make a meal accompanied by the garnishes and a green salad. **MAKES 6 PATTIES**

¼ cup finely diced onion

1 teaspoon minced garlic

¼ cup vegetable oil, divided

2 cups cooked tepary beans

½ teaspoon ground cumin

½ teaspoon dried oregano

Salt and freshly ground black
   pepper

1 egg

1 tablespoon milk (cow, nut, or
   soy)

⅓ cup unbleached all-purpose
   flour

¾ cup dry breadcrumbs

GARNISHES

Mashed avocado

Tomato salsa

Sliced green onions

Sour cream

In a medium frying pan, cook the onion and garlic in 1 tablespoon of the oil until soft. Transfer to the bowl of a food processor. Add the teparies, cumin, oregano, and a sprinkle of salt and pepper. Process until the beans begin to smooth out but are still a little chunky. You do not want a smooth paste.

Beat the egg with the tablespoon of milk, then put the flour, the egg mixture, and the breadcrumbs into separate shallow bowls. Form ¼ cup of the beans into a patty about 2½ inches across. Dip into flour, then egg mixture, then breadcrumbs, putting them on a plate as you finish each.

Heat the remaining 3 tablespoons of oil in a large frying pan. Fry the patties for about 2 minutes on a side, until golden brown. Turn carefully to brown other side. Drain on paper towels.

Serve patties on plates surrounded by the garnishes.

GLUTEN-FREE ALTERNATIVES: For the breading, use any gluten-free flour; substitute dry oat bran for the breadcrumbs.

Tepary Chocolate Brownies

What a great day for chocolate lovers when nutrition scientists announced that dark chocolate is actually good for you — full of antioxidant flavonoids. Goodbye to carob, fine in itself, but no substitute for real chocolate or cocoa powder (which also contains the beneficial flavonoids to varying degrees).

No brownie could ever be called a health food, but these are certainly not empty calories. Besides the chocolate punch, the addition of teparies contributes some great protein. Use whatever color teparies you have.

The recipe is easily made in a food processor. If you don't have one, purée the beans in a blender, then transfer the purée to a bowl and continue mixing in the rest of the ingredients with an electric mixer. These brownies are moist and very chocolaty, and they store well in tins or in the refrigerator.

MAKES SIXTEEN 2-INCH-SQUARE BROWNIES

1 cup cooked tepary beans

2 tablespoons instant coffee

½ cup unsweetened cocoa powder

¾ cup sugar

3 tablespoons canola oil

½ cup unbleached all-purpose flour

2 eggs, well beaten

1½ teaspoons vanilla extract

½ teaspoon salt

Preheat oven to 325 degrees. Grease an 8-inch-square pan. Cut a piece of waxed paper or parchment paper the same size as the bottom of the pan, fit it in, and grease that also.

Process the tepary beans in a food processor until smooth. Add the remaining ingredients and whirl until just combined.

Spread the batter in the prepared baking pan. Bake for 30 to 35 minutes. Remove from oven, cool in pan on rack, then remove brownies and peel off the paper. Cut into 2-inch squares.

Dad's Basic Beans

My father, George Niethammer, was in the food business all his life, managing restaurants and selling groceries. He was an excellent cook, too, specializing in midwestern-style American food. This is his recipe, but made with tepary beans instead of navy beans. Cook the beans in an electric slow cooker, a heavy pot on the stove, or a pressure cooker like Dad used. **MAKES 4 TO 6 SERVINGS**

½ pound tepary beans

1 cup chopped tops and leaves
of celery

1 cup chopped onion

1 carrot, finely grated

1 large clove garlic, minced

½ small, 4-ounce can diced green
chiles

½ teaspoon freshly ground black
pepper

Salt to taste

3 slices bacon

3 or 4 very thin slices onion

Pick through the beans, making sure there are no stones in them, rinse them, and soak them overnight, at least 12 hours, in the refrigerator. To shorten cooking time, you can soak for 2 days in the refrigerator. Drain and rinse.

Transfer soaked beans to a bowl and cover with other ingredients except salt, bacon, and onion slices, and then cover with water.

Cook in a pressure cooker at 15 pounds for 45 minutes or until done, or cook in an electric slow cooker or heavy pot on the stove until tender. When cooked, salt to taste.

Transfer to a baking dish and cover with the slices of bacon and onion. Bake at 350 degrees for 45 minutes.

Wild Greens

When I first began studying wild plants, I despaired of ever being able to tell one green, leafy plant from another. Now as I walk along city streets or desert trails, I have a much different relationship to the plants I pass, whether they are growing up through the sidewalk cracks or hiding under rocks or making an untidy mess in my own front yard. I am on a first-name basis with many of the plants, and although I may not always pick them up and take them home for dinner, I view them not as obnoxious invaders or anonymous ground covers but as living things with which I have at least the possibility of beneficial interaction. I am a person who likes to know my neighbors, be they people or plants.

And the interaction is beneficial—at least on my side. Wild greens are so bursting with vitamins and minerals that they leave iceberg lettuce looking wimpy by comparison. All greens provide calcium, iron, carotene (precursor to vitamin A), riboflavin, folic acid, and vitamin C. One example of the superior vitamin content of wild greens is purslane, which contains four times as much vitamin C as head lettuce, seven times as much calcium, and five times as much iron.

Wild greens usually appear with the early spring and late summer rains. Most of them are ephemerals so, especially in the hot areas, they go through their growth cycle very quickly and are at the fresh and tender stage for only a brief time. Older, flowering greens are most often bitter.

Take care when gathering greens from a spot other than your own yard. Plants near roadways may contain toxins from car exhaust. Greens found near agricultural fields may have been sprayed with pesticides; check with the nearest farmer to made sure the greens are untainted.

At the end of this section, within the amaranth chapter, you'll find a selection of recipes that you can use for any wild green that tastes good when cooked.

Miner's Lettuce (Salad Greens)

Miner's lettuce (*Claytonia perfoliata*) is one of the most delicate and desirable of the wild greens. During the California Gold Rush it was relished by the forty-niners who quickly became weary of their diet of meat and flapjacks. In the hot deserts, miner's lettuce is available only in the very early spring, but in the cool mountains it tends to say fresh longer. It grows in damp places along creeks. To find it, you have to bend down and search under overhanging rocks and dense bushes.

Miner's lettuce has two kinds of leaves, heart shaped and disk shaped, that grow completely around the stem. Unlike the blossoms of other greens, the small white flowers of miner's lettuce do not seem to signal bitterness in the leaves.

Although it can be cooked, cooking this most delicate of greens seems a travesty. The best way to eat it is to sit in the middle of a patch and start munching. However, if you insist on dealing with it in a more civilized manner, be advised that the leaves wilt extremely fast in the heat of a backpack. If you are hiking to a known patch of miner's lettuce with the intent of picking for home use, take along a wide-mouth thermos with an ice cube in it or an insulated bag to protect your harvest.

The lightest sprinkling of vinaigrette is all the dressing you will need on your salad as the leaves taste slightly tangy all by themselves.

Monkey Flower (Salad Greens)

Monkey flower (*Mimulus guttatus* and closely related species) is another early spring green that grows either in the middle of streams or on the banks where the ground is damp. The leaves are about the size of a quarter, round or slightly oval, with toothed edges and sometimes a very slightly hairy surface. They look remarkably like the common houseplant called Creeping Charlie. The flowers resemble tiny yellow snapdragons, but by the time those appear, the plant will be much too bitter to eat.

Like miner's lettuce, monkey flower is best picked very young and fresh and eaten raw with a light dressing.

Purslane (Salad Greens and Cooked)

Purslane (*Portulaca* spp. and *Trianthema portulacastrum*) is a common garden weed and is also found in fields where there is irrigation or after rains. It appears in the summer. The true portulacas are the most desirable and are often sold in the late summer in southwestern grocery stores under the name *verdolagas*.

Both plants grow low to the ground and have pinkish, fleshy stems and succulent leaves, although *Trianthema* is coarser and not as good raw as *Portulaca*. In addition to all the vitamin C, calcium, and iron, purslane also has the most omega-3 fatty acids of any green. This is an important nutrient as our modern diets do not provide enough of it. If that were not enough to make purslane enticing, it also has some of the slippery juices that make certain desert plants helpful for controlling blood sugar for diabetics and the rest of us.

Purslane makes an excellent salad combined with other greens. It is very popular with Mexicans. When I visited some markets outside Mexico City, the market women were selling large, broad bowls of purslane salad. The purslane was chopped, combined with chopped fresh tomatoes and green chiles, dressed with a light vinaigrette, and sprinkled with crumbly *queso fresco* (a dry, fresh cheese). Purslane is also good quickly sautéed with other vegetables.

My friend Roni, who was born into the well-known Capin family in the border town of Nogales, Arizona, taught me to wash purslane in a bowl of water. At the bottom, you'll find some tiny black seeds. Dump the water and seeds into the soil of a flowerpot that you keep watered, and soon you'll have a reliable supply of purslane.

Watercress (Salad Greens and Cooked)

Watercress (*Rorippa nasturtium-aquaticum* and other species) is one of the most widespread and widely recognized wild greens. It is found growing in streams and springs even during the winter if it is not too cold.

Watercress has been known since ancient Greek and Roman times and various writers have disagreed on whether it was a delicious herb or harmful pest.

The debate continues today in the United States. Some Native American populations eat it; others ignore it even when it is easily available. When I was doing research for my first cookbook, I spent an afternoon with a Havasupai woman who lived deep in Supai Canyon at one end of the Grand Canyon. She pointed out many plants and described their uses, but when I was back in my own camp that night, I realized she had not mentioned the watercress that grows so abundantly on the banks of the river that flows through the village. The next day, I hiked back to the village to ask her about it.

"That's food for horses," was her reply.

"But the white people eat it," I prodded. "They even sell it in the grocery stores."

"Well, the Havasupais think it is food for horses," she said with a shake of her head and that was the end of the discussion.

We usually think of watercress simply as an ingredient in salads, but the possibilities for its use are much more extensive, as you can see in the following recipes.

Watercress Salad Dressing

This is good over fresh sliced cucumbers, poached salmon, or cold boiled shrimp. Store leftovers in the refrigerator. **MAKES ABOUT 1½ CUPS**

1 cup packed watercress

1 tablespoon lemon juice

1 tablespoon wine vinegar

¼ cup olive oil

½ teaspoon salt

Pinch dried tarragon

Grating or two of freshly ground
   black pepper

Wash and pick over watercress for any tough or discolored bits. Pat dry with clean dish towel or paper towels.

In a food processor, chop the watercress first, then add remaining ingredients. If using a blender, combine liquid ingredients first, then add watercress and blend until finely chopped.

Oriental Watercress

SERVES 2

2 cups watercress

3 tablespoons peanut or light
   vegetable oil

2 thin slices fresh gingerroot,
   chopped fine

3 green onions, sliced

1 carrot, sliced to pieces the size
   of a matchstick

Soy sauce

Wash and pick over watercress for tough or bruised portions.

Heat oil in wok or large frying pan. Add ginger and green onion and sauté 1 minute. Remove with slotted spoon and reserve.

Sauté carrot until tender. Add watercress, ginger and onion, and toss until watercress is lightly wilted. Shake on a few drops of soy sauce to taste.

Watercress Pineapple Sorbet

This is a sophisticated taste—most children probably would reject it because of the sharpness that contrasts with the sweetness of the pineapple.   MAKES ABOUT 5½ CUPS

⅓ cup watercress leaves

1 small fresh pineapple
   (2½ cups chopped finely)

1½ cups granulated sugar

1 cup water

Juice of 2 large or 3 small limes

Watercress springs for garnish

Wash and pick over the watercress, separating the leaves from the stems, which will be discarded. Set ⅓ cup leaves aside.

Trim rind from pineapple and chop fruit finely. Measure 2½ cups and reserve remainder for another use.

Combine sugar and water in a medium saucepan over medium heat. Stir to dissolve sugar. Remove from heat and cool.

Combine watercress leaves, pineapple, and lime juice in food processor and purée until smooth. Add cooled sugar syrup. Pour into canister of an ice cream maker and process according to manufacturer's directions.

To serve, spoon into pretty glasses and garnish each with a watercress sprig.

Wild Mustard (Salad Greens and Cooked)

The mustard family includes many leafy plants, both wild and cultivated. *Sisymbrium irio* and *Sisymbrium officinale* are two of the tastiest specimens if picked young. *S. irio* has smooth, lobed leaves; the leaves of *S. officinale* are somewhat hairy.

The tender, spicy leaves of wild mustards appear in the deserts as early as January if the weather is wet. They are often so abundant they become a pest. You can deal with them effectively and economically by using them in the recipes within the amaranth chapter.

Wild mustards are among the most widely recognized edible plants; if these two varieties do not occur in your area, ask around at your closest cooperative extension office or college in the spring and you will probably find somebody happy to point out your local edibles.

The small yellow flowers are also edible, with a sharp horseradish-like bite to them. Try one first before using them extensively to see if they suit your taste.

Poverty Weed (Cooked)

Poverty weed (*Monolepis nuttalliana*) came upon its name because so many people have resorted to eating it in times of want. It is unfortunate that the name has stuck, because it makes the plant seem less desirable than its delicate flavor would indicate. It is so high in iron and calcium that it is a healthy choice in good times as well. Perhaps the Spanish term *patota* or the Tohono O'odham word *opon*, which means "lacy," are better names.

The plant comes up with the first spring rains and is found as early as February in low spots, along roadsides and barren areas on mesas, and in places where the soil tends to be alkaline. It grows low to the ground and sometimes in dense thick patches. It has been found as high as 7,500 feet, but usually grows below 3,000 feet.

It can be prepared by boiling, steaming, or stir-frying or can be used in any of the recipes for wild greens within the amaranth chapter.

Lamb's-quarter (Cooked)

This green (*Chenopodium berlandieri, Chenopodium fremontii,* and other species) is sometimes called goosefoot because the shape of the leaves looks like the footprint a goose might leave in a muddy barnyard. That is an easy way to recognize this plant, which appears in March and April in the lower desert and later in summer in the higher mountain areas. I was astonished when several of these plants lived happily through a very hot summer in my desert garden with just a little water now and then.

Because of its abundance and mild flavor, lamb's-quarter is one of the most popular wild foods gathered not just in the West but also throughout the country.

Choose plants less than one foot tall or the new shoots of older plants. The stems are tough, so discard them after you have picked off the succulent leaves. Steam the leaves by placing them in a pot with a tightly fitting lid, add a tablespoon or two of water, and cook over low heat for about five minutes. They are good served simply with butter, vinegar, or a little chile.

If you let the plants grow, they'll produce lots of black seeds that are easily gathered and can be added to baked goods.

Lamb's-quarter is a nutritional powerhouse—a 100-gram serving, around a cup of cooked greens, provides about as much calcium as a cup of cow's milk as well as more vitamin A than a serving of spinach. Use in recipes within the amaranth chapter.

Amaranth (Cooked)

Amaranth (mainly *Amaranthus palmeri*) is a gift of the summer rains in the Southwest. You can curse them as a weed or look on them as free food from Mother Nature. The latter sentiment was the view of Native Americans throughout the Southwest and down into Mexico. Amaranth is a New World plant, but travelers have carried the seeds throughout the world. I purchased a bunch in a northern Nigerian market where it was being sold as "spinach."

Compared to domestic greens and even some other wild greens, amaranth greens are extremely rich in iron, calcium, and niacin as well as vitamins A and C.

The wild amaranth, also called pigweed or *quelite,* is very mild when young—do as the Indians do and pick it when it is no more than a hand high. Use in any of the recipes given in this chapter. When amaranth plants mature, the leaves get tough, but the long tassel-like flowers produce tiny black seeds that are easily gathered.

The amaranth green is a close relative of the grain amaranth found in so many health foods. Amaranth grain and leaves were cultivated and eaten in Mexico at least 7,000 years ago.

The following recipes can be used with wild mustard, poverty weed, lamb's-quarter, or amaranth greens or a mixture. Fill out with garden or commercial greens if you don't have enough for a recipe.

West African Peanut Stew

You'll find this in many countries in West Africa.   MAKES 4 TO 6 SERVINGS

4 cups amaranth or other greens

1 chicken cut into serving-size
   pieces

3 cups water

3 tablespoons oil

2 medium onions, chopped

2 medium tomatoes, chopped

1 tablespoon lime juice

¼ teaspoon ground nutmeg

⅛ teaspoon ground cloves

½ teaspoon cayenne pepper or
   ¼ teaspoon chiltepin powder

1 teaspoon grated orange peel

½ cup peanut butter

2 tablespoons cornstarch

CONDIMENTS

1 cup chopped seeded cucumber

1 cup chopped banana

Shredded coconut

Wash and drain very young amaranth greens. Pick off leaves, discarding woody stems. Set aside.

Place chicken in covered pan, add the 3 cups of water, cover, and simmer until done, about 30 minutes. Remove pot lid and reduce stock or add water to make 2 cups.

In another pot, heat oil and sauté onions over low heat until limp. Add tomatoes, lime juice, nutmeg, cloves, cayenne or chiltepin, and orange peel and bring to a simmer. Add to chicken and stock. Cover and cook just at a simmer until chicken is very tender, about 15 minutes. Turn off heat, add amaranth, and cover (amaranth leaves will wilt).

In a small bowl, blend peanut butter with cornstarch, then add a little water to thin. Stirring, add peanut mixture to stew and cook until sauce thickens. Serve stew over rice and pass the condiments.

Wild Greens Soup

This soup is an intense yet soft green. I often use it as the first course for a dinner party. The little bit of cream adds luxurious richness.   MAKES 4 SERVINGS

8 cups greens

1 tablespoon unsalted butter

2 green onions, chopped with
some of the green

2 tablespoons unbleached
all-purpose flour

2 cups chicken or vegetable stock
or bouillon

1 cup plus 2 tablespoons milk
(cow, soy, or nut)

2 tablespoons cream or
half-and-half

1 lemon

Reserve ¼ cup of the greens. Plunge remaining greens into boiling water for 5 minutes. Drain and press out excess water.

Melt butter in a large heavy saucepan over low heat; add chopped green onions and sauté. When onions are limp, add flour and stir. Cook for a few seconds. Stirring constantly, slowly add 1 cup of stock or bouillon and cook and stir until smooth. Transfer sauce and cooked, drained greens to container of blender and purée. Return to saucepan. Add remaining stock or bouillon, milk, and cream or half-and-half and blend.

Slice 4 thin slices of lemon from center of fruit. Reserve. Squeeze one of remaining halves to produce 1 tablespoon of juice and add to soup. Finely chop reserved ¼ cup of greens.

Ladle soup into four flat soup bowls. Float lemon slices on soup topped with a tiny pile of chopped fresh greens.

Chinese Greens Soup

MAKES 4 TO 6 SERVINGS

¼ pound lean pork

1 tablespoon soy sauce

1 teaspoon oyster sauce

2 teaspoons sesame oil

4 cups chicken broth

1 cup shredded fresh greens

2 green onions, chopped
(including most of the green
tops)

With a sharp knife, slice pork very thin; shred into matchstick-size pieces. Combine meat in a bowl with soy sauce, oyster sauce, and 1 teaspoon of the sesame oil. Marinate 15 minutes.

Meanwhile, bring chicken broth to a boil in a medium saucepan, then reduce heat. Add greens and pork with its marinade. Cook gently for about 7 minutes. Stir in the remaining teaspoon of sesame oil and green onion.

Green Mayonnaise

Use whatever greens you have for this recipe, filling in with spinach or arugula if you don't have enough. Mustard leaves add a little zip.   MAKES 3½ CUPS

1 cup thick yogurt
1½ cup greens
¼ cup chopped fresh parsley
3 green onions, chopped
½ teaspoon horseradish
1 cup mayonnaise
Lemon juice
Salt

If yogurt is not thick, line a colander with cheesecloth and drain the yogurt over a bowl overnight in the refrigerator until it is the consistency of sour cream.

Chop the 1½ cups of greens coarsely.

Bring a large pot of water to a boil and drop in the coarsely chopped greens for a few seconds. Drain, rinse with cold water, and drain again.

Combine yogurt, greens, parsley, chopped green onions, and horseradish in a blender jar or food processor bowl. Blend just to mix.

Put mayonnaise in a bowl and stir in the blended yogurt mixture. Stir in the lemon juice and salt to taste.

Will keep for 4 or 5 days in the refrigerator.

Savory Pastries

These are good with salad for lunch or hearty hors d'oeuvres.   MAKES 8 HORS D'OEUVRES

¾ cup chopped cooked greens
½ cup grated Parmesan cheese
2 green onions, chopped
1 egg, beaten, divided
1 tube of refrigerated crescent roll dough

Preheat oven to 400 degrees.

Press cooked greens into a sieve with the back of a spoon to remove all excess liquid. Combine greens with the cheese, onions, and about half of the beaten egg.

Carefully unroll dough and separate into triangles. Gently stretch each triangle so that is it more or less equilateral. To fill, place a triangle of dough in front of you so that the point is pointing away from you. Place 1/8 of the filling in the middle of the triangle, then roll the triangle over the filling from the long edge toward the point, finishing with the point on top. Press seams together to contain filling. Transfer to an ungreased cookie sheet. Brush tops of pastries with remaining beaten egg.

Bake pastries in preheated oven until well browned on top. Best when hot.

Squares of Green

This is one of my all-time favorite recipes for brunches, christening lunches, and special dinner parties. It was even served at my casual wedding reception. If you don't have enough wild greens, supplement with spinach or any commercial greens. Do use real Parmesan, not the stuff in the cardboard tube.

MAKES 9 SERVINGS

5 cups greens

3 tablespoons unsalted butter

1 small onion, chopped

¼ pound mushrooms, sliced

4 eggs

¼ cup fine dry breadcrumbs

1 can condensed cream of
    mushroom soup

¼ cup grated Parmesan cheese

¼ teaspoon basil

⅛ teaspoon freshly ground
    black pepper

Preheat oven to 325 degrees. Grease a 9-inch-square baking pan.

Plunge greens into boiling water for 1 minute, drain, and chop. Place in wire strainer and press out all liquid. (This liquid is nutritious and can be saved to add to soups and gravies.)

Melt butter in a frying pan over medium heat. Add the onion and mushrooms and sauté until onion is limp.

In a bowl, beat the eggs with a fork, then beat in the breadcrumbs, mushroom soup, half of the cheese, basil, pepper (or more to taste), greens, and onion mixture.

Turn into prepared baking pan and sprinkle with the remaining cheese. Bake uncovered in preheated oven for 35 minutes or until set when touched lightly. Cool. Cut into 3-inch squares.

Serve at room temperature or reheat.

Simple Sautéed Greens with Fruit and Nuts

MAKES ABOUT 4 SERVINGS

6 cups wild greens, mixed
    variety fine

⅓ cup raisins or dried cranberries

1 large thick slice white bread

3 tablespoons olive oil

3 tablespoons piñon nuts or
    chopped pecans

2 garlic cloves, minced

½ lemon

Wash greens and pick leaves from tough stems. Set aside.

Put dried fruit in a small bowl and cover with boiling water; leave to soak for 10 minutes. Drain and pat dry with paper towels.

Cut the bread into small cubes. Heat 2 tablespoons of the olive oil in a wok or frying pan. Quickly fry the bread until golden. Remove and drain croutons on paper towels.

Heat the remaining tablespoon of olive oil and sauté the nuts until they turn golden brown. Add greens and garlic and toss, using tongs, until wilted. Add dried fruit and toss. Squeeze lemon over all, add the croutons, and serve immediately.

Dressed-Up Greens

Almost any wild green that is good cooked is even better in this recipe. **MAKES ABOUT 4 SERVINGS**

6 cups greens

2 tablespoons olive oil

2 cloves garlic, minced

3 tablespoons sliced almonds

½ cup sliced green olives

1 tablespoon capers

Wash and sort greens. Steam until wilted over boiling water. Chop.

Heat oil in skillet and stir in garlic and almonds. Sauté until golden. Add olives, capers, and greens. Serve warm.

Spanakorizo (Greek Greens and Rice)

You can use any mild greens for this recipe. A mixture of greens is fine or supplement with spinach if you don't have enough. For cooking this dish, choose a skillet that has a cover. Serve the finished dish with lemon wedges and crusty bread. **MAKES 6 SIDE-DISH SERVINGS**

1 pound wild greens

2 medium onions, chopped
   coarsely

¼ cup olive oil

1 cup chicken or vegetable broth

2 tablespoons tomato paste

2 tablespoons chopped fresh
   parsley

2 tablespoons dried dill weed

½ cup white rice

Salt and freshly ground black
   pepper

¼ pound crumbled feta cheese

Wash greens and pick leaves from tough stems. Set aside.

In a large skillet over medium heat, sauté onion in olive oil.

Heat broth in a saucepan, then stir in tomato paste. Add this mixture to the onion in the skillet. Add the greens, parsley, dill weed, and rice.

Cover the skillet and simmer over low heat until rice is done, 20 to 30 minutes, adding more broth or water if necessary. Season with salt and pepper to taste and sprinkle with the feta cheese.

. . . .

For another recipe that's very good with wild greens, see also Tomatoes with Greens and Piñon Nuts (page 111).

Flavorings from the Wild

Chiltepins

It seems incongruous that a plant so delicate and lacy, with such diminutive white flowers, could produce the incendiary chiltepin chiles. This plant grows wild on both sides of the U.S.–Mexico border from southern Texas to Baja California.

The tiny chile, about half the size of a pea, has been used to spice foods for at least 8,000 years. It is often called "the mother of all chiles" because it is the closest living relative of the early domesticated chiles.

As a general rule, the hotness of chiles is in inverse proportion to their size. The relative spiciness of chiles is determined by their rating on the Scoville scale, with zero for the mildest bell peppers. The large, fleshy poblanos and Anaheims are generally mild and rate around 500 to 2,500 units, whereas the thumb-sized orange habaneros are 100,000 units or higher. Chiltepins clock in at about 70,000 Scoville units, making them just below the habaneros. An early Spanish priest traveling in chiltepin territory described his first encounter by writing, "I believed I had hellfire in my mouth." Gary Paul Nabhan calls it "the original burning bush."

Chiltepins are a healthy addition to any food, with lots of vitamins A, C, and B_2. However, you probably won't be able to count on chiltepins as a major source of nutrition as the trick in using them is to let just a little do the job.

Practically all chiltepins that you might find for sale are harvested from the wild. The northern limits of these woody perennials are the Sonoran and Chihuahuan Deserts, extending about thirty miles north of the border in Texas, New Mexico, and Arizona. They are endangered in the United States, however, with fewer than fifteen known localities that serve as their natural habitat. This is not surprising as they are very fussy about where they grow. Their habitat must be hot, but it also must be moist and shady. Because they are so rare, chiltepins are protected in Big Bend National Park in Texas and in Coronado National Forest and Organ

Pipe Cactus National Monument in Arizona. There is an unusually high concentration of wild chiltepin plants near Tubac, Arizona, and the U.S. Forest Service has set aside a conservation area to protect them from cattle. Slow Food USA has listed chiltepins in the Ark of Taste, a catalog of delicious foods in danger of extinction.

Growing and Harvesting Your Chiltepins

In the wild, chiltepins grow in "guilds"—that is, in association with other plants. They like the filtered shade of mesquite trees but will also grow under oaks and shrubs. Interestingly, they seem to prefer thorny bushes with red fruit such as hackberry and wolfberry. Besides providing protection from strong sun, the nurse plants shield the chiltepins from frost.

It is possible, however, to grow your own. Linda McKittrick, an urban farmer and wild-food enthusiast, has had good luck propagating chiltepins. She suggests throwing fresh seed under a mesquite or other shady tree or in a pot. Keep the area moist but not soggy and watch for seedlings to pop up. An average chile plant will grow to about four feet, but some in the wild are much larger.

Chiltepins ripen in the fall beginning in September. Pick them only when they separate easily from the plant and are bright red. Dry them on a screen out of direct sunlight and roll them around so that they dry evenly; a mesh fabric screen or light cloth will protect them from birds, who love to eat them. Make sure they are bone dry before storing in jars.

Cooking with Chiltepins

Do wear gloves when handling any chiles—their heat isn't hot enough to blister your hands, but you might forget and touch more sensitive skin on your face and eyes, and that would burn. If you overestimate your tolerance for spiciness and end up with a burning mouth, try milk or ice cream to calm it down. The casein in the milk will attach to and wash away the capsaicin. (Sorry, beer won't help quench the fire, but it might make you feel better about things.) If you do get a fleck of chiltepin in your eye, quickly flush repeatedly with cool water.

Crush chiltepins with a small mortar and pestle. The finer you grind them, the more widely the heat will be disbursed in the food. To cut down on the heat, pick out the seeds. It is a somewhat tedious process—you may end up just deciding to get used to the heat.

Chiltepin Cheese

Homemade farmer-style cheese is becoming a forgotten art. This recipe, devised by Linda McKittrick, is very easy. Thicker types of yogurt, such as Greek, work best. You can also use your homemade yogurt. Serve the cheese on crackers or on cucumber slices or use to stuff celery sticks.   **MAKES 1⅓ CUPS**

1 32-ounce container yogurt

1 tablespoon rock salt

1 teaspoon dried and crushed
   chiltepins, seeds removed
   (add more to taste)

Olive oil

Line a colander with two thicknesses of cheesecloth. Set the colander over a bowl. Spoon the yogurt into the colander and put it all in the refrigerator for 24 hours. Remove from refrigerator, bundle the cheese-cloth, and squeeze out any remaining moisture. Discard the whey accumulated in the bowl or use in baking. Stir in the salt and crushed chiltepins.

Spoon the soft cheese into a jar and cover with olive oil. Store in the refrigerator.

Oaxacan Peanuts

Janos Wilder, the award-winning owner and head chef at his Tucson restaurants Janos, J-Bar, and Downtown Kitchen + Cocktails, devised a much hotter version of this recipe. I've toned down the heat, but once again, the amount of chiltepins to use depends on your tolerance for spiciness. Wilder is an aficionado of local southwestern foods, a love that is reflected in his inventive menus.
MAKES 3 CUPS

2 tablespoons peanut oil

3 cups raw Spanish peanuts with
   the skins on

1 head garlic, broken into cloves,
   unpeeled

½ to 1 teaspoon dried and crushed
   chiltepins, seeds removed

Kosher salt

Lime wedges

Preheat oven to 350 degrees.

Heat the oil over medium-high heat in a large, oven-suitable sauté pan. Add the peanuts, garlic, and chiles. Cook, stirring constantly, for about 5 to 7 minutes until the peanut skins have darkened.

Place in the 350-degree oven and cook the nuts until they are thoroughly roasted, about 10 minutes. Add the salt and mix thoroughly.

Garnish with lime wedges and serve warm.

Chiltepin Salsa

The chiltepins are just a tiny component of this sauce but their presence will be obvious. Feel free to add more if your taste tends to the incendiary. **MAKES ABOUT 7 CUPS**

2 tablespoons vegetable oil

1 medium onion, finely chopped

3 cloves fresh garlic, minced

2 28-ounce cans chopped
  tomatoes

1 bunch fresh cilantro, chopped

1 roasted, peeled poblano chile,
  chopped

½ teaspoon powdered cumin

½ teaspoon dried and crushed
  chiltepins, seeds removed

Salt to taste

In a large saucepan, heat the oil and sauté the onions and garlic until soft. Add the remaining ingredients and simmer for 5 to 10 minutes. Add a little water if it gets too thick.

Transfer to clean jars and refrigerate. If you plan to keep it for more than a week, freeze.

Spicy Peanut Sauce for Noodles

MAKES 3 TO 4 SERVINGS

½ cup Oaxacan Peanuts
  (page 157)

3 to 4 roasted garlic cloves

¾ cup plain yogurt

¼ cup half-and-half

¼ to ½ teaspoon dried and
  crushed chiltepins, seeds
  removed

½ pound spaghetti or fettuccine

Spread out a cotton dishtowel (not terrycloth) and put the peanuts on one half. Fold the other half over and roll the peanuts back and forth to release the skins. Pour the peanuts into a small bowl and shake. The skins will rise to the top and can be skimmed off. If there are more skins, wet your hands and "massage" the nuts. The skins will stick to your hands and can be rinsed off.

Transfer the peanuts to a blender jar and process until they are in small pieces. Add garlic cloves, yogurt, and half-and-half. Taste, and if it needs more spice, add ¼ teaspoon ground chiltepin and taste again before adding more.

Cook pasta until tender, then drain and return to pot. Mix in the peanut sauce. Can be served warm or cold.

Chiltepin Corn Scones

These are good served with a cooling or creamy soup such as cucumber or gazpacho. If you like really spicy foods, you can double the amount of chiltepins. **MAKES 12 SCONES**

2 cups unbleached all-purpose
   flour

¾ cup yellow cornmeal

1 tablespoon baking powder

½ teaspoon salt

1 teaspoon dried and crushed
   chiltepins, seeds removed

½ teaspoon powdered cumin

6 tablespoons cold unsalted
   butter

¼ pound cheddar or longhorn
   cheese, shredded (2 cups
   lightly packed)

2 large eggs

1 tablespoon milk (cow, nut, or
   soy)

1 small can (8.75 ounces) creamed
   corn

Preheat oven to 400 degrees. Oil a 12- by 15-inch baking sheet.

Combine flour, cornmeal, baking powder, salt, chiltepins, and cumin in a bowl or a food processor. Stir or whirl until combined. Add cold butter and rub in with your fingers if using a bowl or whirl in the food processor until mixture forms coarse crumbs. Stir in cheese or add to processor and whirl for a few seconds.

In a separate bowl, beat eggs until frothy. Remove 1 tablespoon of the egg to a small bowl and add the tablespoon of milk. Set aside.

Add creamed corn to remaining eggs and stir to combine. Add the corn mixture to the flour mixture and stir or whirl just until combined and evenly moistened.

Turn mixture out onto a floured board and knead a few times until dough forms a cohesive ball. Divide dough in half. Form each half into a patty about 6 inches in diameter and ¾ inch thick. Transfer each patty to the oiled baking sheet, separating them by several inches. Using a knife, cut each patty almost through into 6 equal wedges. Brush with the reserved egg and milk mixture.

Bake in preheated oven about 20 to 22 minutes or until nicely browned.

Easy Chocolate-Chile Ice Cream

This recipe combines two of the iconic flavors of Mexico: chile and chocolate. Some version of this is always a great hit at chile festivals throughout the Southwest.   MAKES A HALF GALLON

½ gallon commercial chocolate ice cream

¼ to ½ teaspoon dried and crushed chiltepins, seeds removed

½ teaspoon ground chipotle chiles

Transfer the ice cream from the carton in large clumps and place in a flat baking pan to soften evenly. (If you try to soften it in the carton, the outside will get too soft while the interior stays hard.)

Meanwhile, crush the chiltepins in a small mortar, removing the seeds. Sprinkle the crushed chiltepins and ground chipotles over the ice cream and stir to combine. Repack into the carton or transfer to a bowl and refreeze.

Chocolate-Chiltepin Cupcakes with Cool/Hot Cream Cheese Frosting

This is the way to zip up a chocolate cupcake! Linda McKittrick, urban farmer and wild-food forager, developed this recipe. She points out that an interesting sensation occurs on your tongue when the cool of the mint in the frosting interacts with the heat of the chile.   MAKES 12 CUPCAKES

1 cup milk (cow, nut, or soy)

1 teaspoon apple cider vinegar

¼ cup honey

⅓ cup safflower oil

1 teaspoon vanilla extract

1 cup unbleached all-purpose flour

⅓ cup cocoa

¼ teaspoon dried and crushed chiltepins, seeds removed

¾ teaspoon baking soda

¾ teaspoon baking powder

¼ teaspoon salt

Preheat oven to 350 degrees and line 12 cupcake cups with paper liners.

Whisk together the milk and vinegar in a large bowl; set aside to allow time to curdle. Once curdled, add the honey, oil, and vanilla extract and blend well.

Sift the dry ingredients together and slowly add to the wet mixture, stirring between additions. Divide batter among the cups, filling each about ¾ full.

Bake in preheated oven for 18 to 20 minutes.

Cool/Hot Cream Cheese Frosting

Sifting the seeds out of the chile flakes will help keep the heat level constant over a day or two, but if you want the heat to grow hotter, leave seeds in. If you are going to serve the cupcakes immediately, you can save time by not sifting.   **MAKES ENOUGH TO FROST 12 CUPCAKES**

2 8-ounce packages cream cheese, softened

2 tablespoons unsalted butter, softened

1 teaspoon vanilla extract

1 teaspoon mint extract

1 teaspoon chocolate extract

1 tablespoon cocoa powder

¾ cup powdered sugar

1 to 2 tablespoons milk (cow, nut, or soy)

⅛ to ¼ teaspoon dried and crushed chiltepins, seeds removed

12 sprigs of fresh mint (for garnish)

Combine all ingredients except the fresh mint in a food processor bowl and mix until well combined. Add just 1 tablespoon of milk at first, adding the rest by teaspoons if needed to thin.

Frost cupcakes and garnish each with a small sprig of fresh mint.

For another recipe with chiltepin, see Three Sisters Soup (page 129).

Mexican Oregano

Several different plants go by the name "Mexican oregano." Although it seems none of them grow wild in the United States, several species of *Lippia,* which are in the same family as lemon verbena, grow in northern mainland Mexico and in Baja California and the islands in the Gulf of California. Local inhabitants of these areas, including the Seri and Tarahumara, have used it extensively as both a flavoring and a green. The plant is used by local herbalists as a medicine, sometimes in the form of a tea to soothe sore throats and coughs. The Seris harvest the oregano leaves very carefully, stripping them from the twigs rather than cutting the twigs. That way the leaves will regenerate more quickly.

Also called Mexican oregano is *Poliomintha longiflora,* which is grown as a garden ornamental throughout the West. It is a lovely plant that likes heat and drips with tubular lavender blossoms in the summer.

The leaves of both plants are much stronger than Mediterranean oregano—they are so strong they leave a tingle on your tongue. The flavor comes from a phenol called carvacrol, one of the components of oregano oil. While Mediterranean oregano is about 2 percent carvacrol, Mexican varieties tend to be 3 to 4 percent. In addition to the strong oregano flavor, there's a little something extra there. Maybe a taste expert would call it "floral notes"; others have called it lemony.

Mexican oregano is also high in antioxidants—much more per weight than other berries, even blueberries.

Lippia is listed in Slow Food USA's Ark of Taste (where it is called desert oregano), a catalog of delicious foods in danger of extinction.

Use Mexican oregano anywhere you would use Mediterranean oregano—just be careful with the amounts. Mexican oregano is available in the Mexican spice section of most markets and can be found online.

Here are a few recipes to get you started. See also the recipes for the sauce for Molly's Mesquite Tamales (page 90) and Three Sisters Soup (page 129).

Easy Salsa

This is a good dipping sauce for chips, but really shines as a sauce for huevos rancheros. To use it for that, soften corn tortillas in a little oil, smear with mashed pinto or tepary beans, then top with eggs cooked as you wish (over easy is traditional). Finish by surrounding with this great salsa. MAKES ABOUT 2¾ CUPS

½ cup chopped onion

1 tablespoon olive oil

1 large clove garlic, minced

1 can (14.5 ounces) chopped
  tomatoes

¼ cup diced green chiles

½ to 1 teaspoon dried Mexican
  oregano

¼ cup cilantro leaves

1 to 2 teaspoons minced jalapeño
  (optional)

In a medium heavy-bottomed saucepan over low-medium heat, sauté the chopped onion in the olive oil until it begins to soften.

Add the minced garlic and cook until translucent.

Add the remaining ingredients and simmer gently for 5 to 7 minutes to let flavors meld.

Southwestern Green Sauce

When you need to add some zip to grilled chicken or fish, or a slice of grilled tofu, turn to this sauce to add flavor and interest. Or stir it into a pan of sautéed summer squash. Be sure to pluck just the parsley leaves; once the leaves wilt in the sauce the smallest stems are very prominent.   **MAKES 2 SERVINGS**

½ cup sliced green onions

1 tablespoon olive oil

1 teaspoon minced garlic

1 cup parsley leaves

1 tablespoon green chiles

¼ teaspoon minced jalapeño
  (optional)

1 tablespoon dried Mexican
  oregano

½ teaspoon lime juice

In a medium frying pan, over medium-low heat, sauté the green onions in the olive oil until limp.

Add the minced garlic and continue cooking until all pieces are translucent.

Add the parsley leaves, green chiles, jalapeño if desired, and Mexican oregano and sauté until the leaves are cooked, just a few minutes. Sprinkle lime juice over sauce and serve.

Juniper Berries

Juniper trees (genus *Juniperus*) in several species are found throughout the West, usually at elevations of at least 3,000 feet. They frequently grow with piñon pines—both are smallish trees with a form like a bush rather than a single trunk tree with the foliage on top. The branches are aromatic firewood, making juniper smoke the defining fragrance of winter in northern New Mexico.

What we call juniper berries are actually small cones. They are green the first year and then change to purplish blue the second year. Once gathered, they should be dried. If you don't wish to gather them yourself, there are many online sources for juniper berries. They have been described as being pungent and piney. The flavor doesn't last on the shelf for years—they tend to become rather tasteless after a year or so.

Pregnant women and people suffering from kidney ailments should avoid juniper berries. That's because one of juniper's active ingredients is terpinen-4-ol, a known diuretic that causes irritation to kidney functions, although by the time the berries have been dried the effect is diminished.

Spanish scientists have experimented with an extract of juniper and found it has potential to lower blood sugar in diabetics and that it also has antiviral properties. The active principal in juniper is podophyllotoxin, which is the pharmacological precursor for the important chemotherapy drug etoposide.

The ashes of juniper have been used by Hopi Indian cooks to keep blue corn from turning gray when cooked. Usually Hopis mix some ashes in water and then strain the water into the corn batter.

While juniper is not widely used, the flavor is familiar to anyone who has ever had a drink of gin—juniper berries are used along with other herbs to impart the recognizable flavor to this alcohol.

A folk tale holds that planting a juniper tree by the front door will keep away witches. Couldn't hurt.

Juniper Pork

The flavors of juniper and pork were made for each other. If you've made your own gin from the recipe on page 171, use that. If not, commercial gin will do. The alcohol in the wine and gin will cook off.

MAKES 4 SERVINGS

1 onion, chopped

3 tablespoons olive oil

1 pound pork stew meat

1 cup chicken broth

1 cup red wine

¼ cup gin

16 dried juniper berries, crushed

1 teaspoon fresh thyme leaves
   or ½ teaspoon dried

Sauté onion in a large frying pan in 2 tablespoons of the olive oil. When soft, put into a Dutch oven or electric slow cooker.

Add the additional tablespoon of olive oil to the frying pan and brown the pork stew meat, turning until brown on all sides. Transfer the meat to the Dutch oven or slow cooker.

In the frying pan, combine the chicken broth, red wine, gin, and juniper berries and bring to a boil. Pour over the meat.

Cook over low heat in the Dutch oven or on high in the slow cooker for 2 to 3 hours or until the meat is tender. If you are cooking in a Dutch oven, the sauce will probably have cooked down. If cooking in a slow cooker, ladle out the broth to a saucepan and cook over medium heat to reduce until a gravy-like consistency.

Red Cabbage with Juniper Berries

This is an Eastern European–style vegetable dish. It can be made ahead and reheated with no loss of quality. Add more juniper berries for a stronger flavor. Add a few cut-up sausages to make a more complete meal. **MAKES 4 TO 6 SERVINGS**

1 tablespoon olive or vegetable oil

1 onion, chopped

1 Granny Smith apple, peeled, cored, and thinly sliced

3 cups shredded red cabbage

6 dried juniper berries, crushed

¼ cup red wine vinegar

¼ cup firmly packed brown sugar

Salt and freshly ground black pepper to taste

In a wok or large frying pan with a cover, heat the oil and sauté the onion and apples until onion is wilted. Add the cabbage and the juniper berries, turn heat to low, cover, and cook for about 5 minutes, stirring occasionally.

Uncover and add the red wine vinegar, brown sugar, and salt and pepper. Cook another 5 minutes until cabbage is tender. Serve hot.

Juniper Berry–Chili Rub for Meat

This recipe was developed by Molly Beverly, food services director at Prescott College. She gathers berries from the alligator juniper (*Juniperus deppeana*) native to Arizona and cautions that there is a wide variation in flavor between plants and also when gathered at different times of the year.

MAKES ENOUGH FOR 3 TO 4 POUNDS OF CHICKEN, TURKEY, OR PORK

½ ounce (heaping ¼ cup) dried
    juniper berries
2 tablespoons chili powder, mild
    or hot, per your taste
1 teaspoon Mexican oregano,
    whole leaf (page 163)
1 teaspoon ground cumin
2 teaspoons unsweetened cocoa
    powder
2 teaspoons kosher salt
4 large, fat cloves garlic
4 tablespoons olive oil
Water as needed

Using a blender, grind juniper berries. Add remaining ingredients and grind all to a paste, adding water to keep liquid moving.

Rub into meat and allow to marinate, refrigerated, for 4 to 6 hours. Roast, basting with excess marinade from pan.

Artisanal Juniper Gin

Although there are hundreds of varieties of beer available to buyers, thousands of home brewers still enjoy making their own—finding pleasure in producing a signature flavor. So why not artisanal gin? Forget the bathtub, you can use a jar. (I have read that actually, during Prohibition, "bathtub gin" was not mixed in the bathtub—it was just that the containers it was made in were so large they would not fit under the kitchen faucet; thus they were filled in the bathtub.) Start with just a pint so you can adjust the seasoning to your taste in subsequent batches.

2 cups inexpensive vodka

2 teaspoons dried juniper berries

¼ teaspoon coriander seed

⅛ teaspoon allspice

⅛ teaspoon fennel seed

2 green cardamom pods

2 black peppercorns

½ bay leaf, torn into pieces

½-inch sprig fresh rosemary
   (just the tip)

One 1- by 3-inch strip fresh
   grapefruit peel or lemon peel,
   sliced into 3 strips

⅛ teaspoon culinary lavender
   buds or small sprig fresh
   lavender

Put the vodka into a pint jar leaving just a little room. Add the juniper berries and remaining spices, herbs, and fruit strip and let infuse all day.

Strain through an unbleached coffee filter. Sip and enjoy, combine it with a whiff of vermouth for a martini, or mix with tonic.

Lemonade Bush (Sumac)

This common small bush goes by the name sumac, lemonade bush, squawberry, or skunkbush because of the smell of the leaves. It produces small red fruits with a strong lemony flavor. The fruits have been used by many Indian groups to make a beverage—in recent years they have jokingly referred to it as Indian Kool-Aid. Many years ago the Yavapai leader Grace Mitchell told me that her people had sweetened the juice with baked mescal (agave) pulp, but you can use honey, sugar, or agave syrup.

The small, flattish fruits, only about a quarter inch long, are slightly fuzzy and sticky. The fruits are not juicy, which makes them easier to dry for storage. The sour flavor comes from malic acid.

When preparing the dry fruits for use in these recipes, grind them as finely as possible, then sift, using a fine sieve, to obtain small flakes. The coarse pieces that remain in the sieve can be used for Rhus Juice (page 174) instead of the flakes.

The scientific name *Rhus trilobata* tells something about the appearance of the bush—the leaves appear in threes. The bushes are rarely over six feet tall and grow throughout the West at altitudes of 2,500 to 5,000 feet.

Rhus Juice

Sipped hot or cold, this refreshing liquid has the taste of the desert. This is the easiest recipe for using lemonade-bush (sumac) fruits. However, of course, first you must find, pick, dry, and crush the fruits. I like foods that are a bit tart, so I find this acceptable without sweetening. Add a bit of sugar or agave syrup if you would like it sweeter.   **MAKES 1 QUART**

¼ cup dried sumac flakes

1 quart water

Place the sumac flakes in a bowl and pour the water over them. Let sit for an hour or so. Strain through a very fine mesh strainer. To remove more of the solids, strain through muslin.

Zahtar

This spice mix is of Middle Eastern origin, but is a wonderful way to use the tangy southwestern sumac fruits. Serve with warm pita triangles and a small dish of good olive oil. Dip the pita into the olive oil and then into the zahtar. You can also sprinkle the mixture on a green salad to add flavor and texture.

MAKES ABOUT ⅓ CUP

2 tablespoons dried sumac flakes

1 tablespoon dried thyme leaves

2 tablespoons toasted sesame
  seeds

1 teaspoon coarse salt

½ teaspoon freshly ground black
  pepper

Mix all ingredients in a bowl. Transfer to a jar for storage.

Sumac Chicken

MAKES 2 TO 4 SERVINGS

1 pound boneless chicken pieces
(about 2 cups)

¼ cup dried sumac flakes

1 tablespoon dried basil flakes

1½ teaspoons crushed coriander
seed

½ teaspoon salt

½ teaspoon freshly ground black
pepper

Pinch cayenne pepper (optional)

Juice of ½ lemon

2 to 3 tablespoons olive oil

⅓ cup water

Cut the chicken into pieces approximately 1 inch square—odd-shaped pieces are fine—and put 2 cups of the pieces in a bowl. Mix the sumac flakes, basil flakes, coriander, salt, pepper, and cayenne, if using, together in a small bowl. Sprinkle over the chicken pieces and stir until evenly coated. Add lemon juice and stir.

Heat a little of the olive oil in a small wok or frying pan. Sauté about a quarter of the chicken pieces until nearly done. Transfer to a clean plate or bowl. Continue sautéing the chicken in batches, using a small amount of the oil for each batch. You may have to clean the pan between batches if the coating begins to collect on the pan.

When all the pieces are browned, put all back in the pan, add ⅓ cup water, cover, and simmer for a few minutes until you are sure all the chicken pieces are thoroughly cooked. Remove the cover and reduce the sauce.

High Desert Fish

We should all eat more fish—but some folks don't like anything with a fishy taste. The problem with mild-flavored fish is that it is so mild as to be uninteresting. This coating can stand up to flavorful varieties of fish and add interest to milder types such as tilapia. **MAKES 2 SERVINGS**

3 tablespoons dried sumac flakes

¾ teaspoon garlic powder

¾ teaspoon dried dill weed

¼ teaspoon freshly ground black
  pepper

1 tablespoon olive oil

2 fish filets (about ½ pound each)

Combine the sumac flakes, garlic powder, dill weed, and black pepper in a small bowl. Add the olive oil and stir until well combined.

Pat the mixture on both sides of the filets. Grill or broil. Thin filets will be done quickly so watch closely and don't burn.

Double Pucker Muffins

These muffins have a double dose of tart flavor—from lemons and from a sumac topping. Lemon-flavored yogurt adds an additional punch. **MAKES 12 MUFFINS**

2 tablespoons dried sumac flakes

1 tablespoon sugar

1 cup unbleached all-purpose flour

1 cup whole wheat flour

½ cup sugar

1 teaspoon baking powder

½ teaspoon baking soda

¼ teaspoon salt

2 large eggs

3 tablespoons unsalted butter, melted

1 tablespoon grated lemon rind (about 2 lemons)

¼ cup fresh lemon juice (about 1 lemon)

1 cup low-fat, lemon-flavored yogurt

Preheat oven to 400 degrees. Grease muffin pan or coat with nonstick cooking spray.

Grind the sumac flakes until fine in mortar or electric coffee grinder. Combine with the tablespoon of sugar and set aside.

In a large bowl, combine flours, the ½ cup sugar, baking powder, baking soda, and salt. Mix well.

In a separate small bowl, beat eggs until light. Stir in the melted butter, grated lemon rind, lemon juice, and yogurt until combined. Add wet ingredients to dry ingredients, stirring until just combined. Do not overstir.

Fill each muffin cup half full. Using half the sumac-sugar mixture, sprinkle a bit in each section. Top with remaining muffin batter and sprinkle the remaining sumac mixture on the top of each muffin. Bake for 15 minutes.

Wild Mint

The wild western mint is Mentha arvensis. It is found only at altitudes above 5,000 feet and in wet places. Some southwestern Indian groups arranged special gathering trips to areas where they knew mint grew. A Taos Indian woman friend told me she wrapped fresh fish in mint leaves before baking it in her adobe oven.

If you find some to gather, just snip off the stalks. Leave the roots in the ground to produce more mint.

Fresh Mint Tea

This is refreshing on a hot summer day. Experiment with combinations of teas and juices.
Herb tea bags in place of the black tea can be delicious. **MAKES 2½ QUARTS**

2 black-tea tea bags

2 green-tea tea bags

½ cup packed fresh mint leaves

3 cups boiling water

1 cup sugar

6 cups water

½ cup orange juice

¼ cup lemon juice

Sprigs of mint

Orange slices

Put tea bags and the ½ cup of packed fresh mint in a 3-quart heatproof pitcher, add the 3 cups of boiling water, and steep until cool. Discard bags and mint leaves.

While tea is steeping, make a simple syrup by combining the 1 cup of sugar and 6 cups of water in a small saucepan and cooking until sugar is dissolved. Cool.

Add orange juice, lemon juice, and sugar syrup to tea mixture. Stir and serve over ice. Garnish with sprigs of mint and orange slices.

Watermelon Agua Fresca

Drinks like this are popular in Mexico. If your watermelon is very sweet, use half the sugar and taste.
You can always add more. **MAKES 8 SERVINGS**

4 cups cubed seeded watermelon

½ cup water

2 limes

48 fresh mint leaves

½ cup white sugar, or to taste

4 slices lime

Ice

Purée the watermelon and water in a blender until smooth.

Halve the limes and squeeze into a shallow bowl. Remove any seeds. Grate ¼ teaspoon of the lime rind and add to the juice. Add half of the mint leaves (24) and crush into the juice with the back of a spoon or a fork. Remove mint leaves and add juice to the watermelon water. Add sugar to taste.

Fill each of 8 glasses with ice. Cut the lime slices in half. Place a half lime slice into each glass along with 3 mint leaves. Pour in the watermelon water and stir before serving.

Minted Goat Cheese

This is a good spread to offer with crackers for appetizers.

MAKES ABOUT 1 ¼ CUPS

1 4-ounce package goat cheese

5 tablespoons chopped fresh mint

½ cup chopped roasted red
  peppers

½ teaspoon grated lemon or lime
  rind

Put goat cheese in a small bowl and stir to soften. Add remaining ingredients and stir to combine.

Easy Mint Sauce

You need not pick the leaves off the mint stems for this since you will be discarding the mint at the end of the process. Don't turn your back on this while it is cooking as it can burn quickly.

This is excellent on meats or on a fruit salad.   MAKES ABOUT ½ CUP

½ cup white wine vinegar

½ cup sugar

½ cup fresh mint

Combine all ingredients in a small saucepan. Cook over medium heat, watching constantly. When the mixture thickens, strain through a wire sieve, Discard the mint.

Transfer sauce to a clean glass jar and store in the refrigerator.

A FINAL WORD

So now we have explored together through many recipes how the Southwest's deserts and mountains can provide wonderful foods for our tables. These 23 plants are only the barest beginning of what Mother Nature has provided for us. Since Wendy Hodgson has told us that the Sonoran Desert has 540 edible wild plants, that leaves 517 more to be investigated in that region alone. Then there are even more plants in the other ecosystems found in the grasslands and mountainous regions throughout the Southwest and the Chihuahua Desert and the hill-country regions of Texas.

Clearly there remain years of pleasure and investigation for the adventurous cook, not only in finding new plants to harvest, but also in devising additional recipes for the 23 plants discussed here.

For those interested in learning more, here are some groups that have formed to research, enjoy, and share the process of finding our way back to a way of eating that is saner and honors our place in our own foodshed. The sources section and further reading list detail books and online resources that deal with the subject in various ways.

Organizations

These organizations are not all dedicated exclusively to local foods or medicines, but they include that interest as a component of their work.

Arizona Ethnobotanical Research Association
107 N. San Francisco Street, Suite 1
Flagstaff, AZ 86001
azethnobotany@hotmail.com

Desert Harvesters
www.desertharvesters.org
Lots of information on mesquite. Grind mesquite pods with their hammermills throughout the Tucson area.

Dreaming New Mexico
A Bioneers Project
1607 Paseo de Peralta, Suite 3
Santa Fe, NM 87501
www.dreamingnewmexico.org
877-246-6337

Native Seeds/SEARCH
Southwestern Endangered Aridland Resource Clearing House
3061 N. Campbell Avenue
Tucson, AZ 85719
www.nativeseeds.org

Sabores sin Fronteras/Flavors without Borders
www.saboresfronteras.com
www.saboressinfronteras@gmail.com

Santa Cruz Valley Heritage Alliance
Vanessa Bechtol, Executive Director
www.santacruzheritage.org
P.O. Box 3445
Tucson, AZ 85722

Al and Jane Smoake
A & J Family Farms
505-507-0991; 505-515-7654
aandjfamilyfarm@yahoo.com
www.socorro-nm.com/a&j-farms.htm

SOURCES

xiv   *For some in the [food] movement* Michael Pollan, "The Food Movement, Rising," *New York Review of Books,* June 10, 2010.

xvi   *If every U.S. citizen ate just one meal a week* Steven L. Hopp, "Oily Food," in *Animal, Vegetable, Miracle,* Barbara Kingsolver (New York: Harper Perennial 2007), 5.

4   *[P]rovides 13 percent of the recommended daily allowance of vitamins A and C* http://nutritiondata.self.com.

5   *An effective amount can be as little as 100 grams daily* Miguel Angel Gutierrez, "Medicinal Use of the Latin Food Staple Nopales: The Prickly Pear Cactus", *Nutrition Bytes,* 4 (1998), no. 2.

24   *"No!" Marquita replied with a strain of horror in her voice* Gary Paul Nabhan, *The Desert Smells Like Rain* (Tucson: University of Arizona Press, 1982), 27.

24   *"[R]ainhouse" full of wind, water, and seeds* Anna Humphreys and Susan Lowell, *Saguaro: The Desert Giant* (Tucson: Rio Nuevo Publishers, 2002), 38.

24   *[B]ecame so corpulent after eating huge quantities* Edward F. Castetter and Willis H. Bell, "The Aboriginal Utilization of the Tall Cacti in the American Southwest," *University of New Mexico Bulletin, Biology Series* 5 (1937), no. 1, 31.

24   *[E]ach whole fruit contains about 34 calories* Winifred Ross, "The Present Day Dietary Habits of the Papago Indians," master's thesis, University of Arizona, Tucson, 1941.

25   *As the story is commonly told* Frank Crosswhite, "The Annual Saguaro Harvest and Crop Cycle of the Papago, with Reference to Ecology and Symbolism," *Desert Plants* 2 (1980), 2–61.

40   *[A] 100-gram serving (50 freshly baked buds)* Wendy Hodgson, *Food Plants of the Sonoran Desert* (Tucson: University of Arizona Press, 2001), 107.

49   *The fruits set in the summer* Jonathan DuHamel, "Edible Desert Plants—

Barrel Cactus Fruit," *WryHeat*, August 1, 2009, http://tucsoncitizen.com/wryheat/2009/08/01/edible-desert-plants-barrel-cactus-fruit/

50   *"[T]he taste varies from intolerable to barely tolerable"* Wendy Hodgson, *Food Plants of the Sonoran Desert* (Tucson: University of Arizona Press, 2001), 118.

68   *Bellotas are another food included in Slow Food USA's Ark of Taste* Click on "Nuts" under "All Products" at http://www.slowfoodusa.org/index.php/programs/details/ark_of_taste/

113   *[C]hia seeds "could well be nature's perfect food"* Christina Pirello, "Change Your Life with Chia," Huffington Post (huffingtonpost.com), February 2, 2010.

155   *"I believed I had hell-fire in my mouth"* and *"the original burning bush"* G. P. Nabhan, "Chiltepins! Wild Spice of the American Southwest," *El Palacio* 84 (1978), 30.

156   *Slow Food USA has listed chiltepins in the Ark of Taste* Click on "Vegetables" under "All Products" at http://www.slowfoodusa.org/index.php/programs/details/ark_of_taste/

163   Lippia *is listed in Slow Food USA's Ark of Taste* Click on "Herbs & Spices" under "All Products" at http://www.slowfoodusa.org/index.php/programs/details/ark_of_taste/

FURTHER READING

Further reading on eating local and food traditions:

Ayerza, Ricardo, Jr., and Wayne Coates. *Chia: Rediscovering a Forgotten Crop of the Aztecs* (Tucson: University of Arizona Press, 2005).

Bendrick, Lou. *Eat Where You Live: How to Find and Enjoy Fantastic Local and Enjoyable Food No Matter Where You Live* (Seattle: Skipstone Press, 2008).

Beranbaum, Rose Levy. *The Cake Bible*, 8th edition (New York: William Morrow, 1988).

Clark, Amalia Ruiz. *Amalia's Special Mexican Dishes*, revised edition (Oracle, AZ: Gila River Designs, 1994).

Clark, Mary Ann, and Shannon Scott, compilers. *From Furrow to Fire: Recipes from the Native Seeds/SEARCH Community* (Tucson: Native Seeds/SEARCH, 2005).

Corriher, Shirley O. *CookWise: The Secrets of Cooking Revealed* (New York: William Morrow, 1997).

Desert Harvesters. *Eat Mesquite! A Cookbook* (Tucson: 2011).

Hodgson, Wendy. *Food Plants of the Sonoran Desert* (Tucson: University of Arizona Press, 2001).

Kingsolver, Barbara. *Animal, Vegetable, Miracle: A Year of Food Life* (New York: Harper Perennial, 2008).

Larousse Gastronomique (New York: Clarkson Potter, 2001).

Nabhan, Gary Paul. *Coming Home to Eat: The Pleasures and Politics of Local Foods* (New York: W. W. Norton and Company, reissue 2009).

———. *The Desert Smells Like Rain: A Naturalist in Papago Indian Country* (New York: North Point Press, 1987).

———, ed. *Renewing America's Food Traditions: Savoring and Saving the Continent's Most Endangered Foods* (White River Junction, VT: Chelsea Green Publishing, 2008).

Niethammer, Carolyn. *American Indian Cooking: Recipes from the Southwest* (Lincoln: University of Nebraska Press/Bison Books, 1999).

———. *The Prickly Pear Cookbook* (Tucson: Rio Nuevo Publishers, 2004).

Pollan, Michael. *In Defense of Food: An Eater's Manifesto* (New York: Penguin, 2009).

Rombauer, Irma S., and Marion Rombauer Becker. *Joy of Cooking* (Indianapolis/New York: Bobbs-Merrill Company, 1964).

Sharpe, John. *La Posada's Turquoise Room Cookbook* (Winslow, AZ: JPS Desert Oasis, 2008).

Tohono O'odham Community Action with Mary Paganelli and Frances Manuel. *From I'itoi's Garden: Tohono O'odham Food Traditions* (2010).

Tull, Delena. *Edible and Useful Plants of Texas and the Southwest* (Austin: University of Texas Press, 1999).

Vileisis, Ann. *Kitchen Literacy: How We Lost Knowledge of Where Food Comes From and Why We Need to Get It Back* (Washington, DC: Island Press, 2007).

For medicinal information:

Greenhouse, Ruth. "The Iron and Calcium Content of Some Traditional Pima Foods and the Effects of Preparation Methods," master of science thesis (Tempe: Arizona State University, 1979).

Kane, Charles. *Herbal Medicine of the American Southwest: The Definitive Guide* (Oracle, AZ: Lincoln Town Press, 2009).

Kay, Margarita Artschwager. *Healing with Plants in the American and Mexican West* (Tucson: University of Arizona Press, 1996).

Moore, Michael. *Medicinal Plants of the Desert and Canyon West* (Santa Fe: Museum of New Mexico Press, 1990).

———. *Medicinal Plants of the Mountain West* (Santa Fe: Museum of New Mexico Press, 2003).

INDEX

ABOUT THE AUTHOR

Carolyn Niethammer learned to love the Southwest while growing up outside the little mountain town of Prescott, Arizona, where there were more cattle than people in the rural county. She has spent her life writing about the foods and people of the region. Her cookbooks include *American Indian Cooking: Recipes from the Southwest,* a compilation of edible wild plants; *The Tumbleweed Gourmet,* modern recipes for edible wild plants; *The Prickly Pear Cookbook,* on all the uses of cactus pads and fruits, and *The New Southwest Cookbook,* bringing together recipes from famous restaurants and resorts. Her greatest joy is devising recipes for foods she has gathering in the wild or grown in her garden.

In her travel guide *West of Paradise: Exploring Southeastern Arizona,* Niethammer shared her knowledge and love of the area with newcomers and old-timers alike. She has also published three books on Native American women.

Niethammer lives in Tucson, Arizona, with her husband, Ford Burkhart.